ZANE PRESENTS

MAKE IT
LAST
FOREVER

THE DOS AND DON'TS

Dear Reader:

Keith Sweat is a legend among men, known for his deep, mesmerizing voice, his tantalizing lyrics, his charisma, and his popular nightly syndicated radio show "The Sweat Hotel." It should come as no surprise that he understands all about the dos and don'ts of falling in love, making love, and knowing when to walk away from unhealthy love. In *Make it Last Forever*, he gives readers his insight, both from a professional and personal viewpoint.

Life can be hard to figure out sometimes, especially when it comes to understanding the mindset and behavior of others. Having helped thousands of his listeners analyze and improve their relationships, Sweat is a life coach with a cutting-edge demeanor. There is nothing coated with sugar in this book. And it is refreshing to hear a man's side because so many women today tend to believe that men are void of feelings. Not so, and *Make it Last Forever* proves that while women are loving men, they are also loving back. At the end of the day, everyone wants reciprocity, companionship, and a peaceful existence to come home to. This book is a catalyst to achieve those things in a mature, responsible, and considerate manner.

As always, thanks for your support of myself and the authors that I bring you under Strebor Books. We strive to bring you the most prolific writers, paramount concepts, and unsurpassed material that will spark both thought and discussion. We appreciate the love and I am confident that you will enjoy Keith Sweat's intriguing perspective into what makes us all tick, what we all fear, and what we all need and expect from our mates. You can find me on Facebook at Author Zane and on Twitter at Planetzane..

Blessings,

Zane

Zane
Publisher
Strebor Books International
www.simonandschuster.com/streborbooks

ZANE PRESENTS

MAKE IT LAST FOREVER

THE DOS AND DON'TS

KEITH SWEAT

SBI

STREBOR BOOKS

NEW YORK LONDON TORONTO SYDNEY

Strebor Books
P.O. Box 6505
Largo, MD 20792
http://www.streborbooks.com

This book is a work of nonfiction.

ISBN 978-1-59309-407-2
ISBN 978-1-4516-5577-3 (ebook)
LCCN 2011938326

First Strebor Books trade paperback edition February 2013

Cover design: www.mariondesigns.com
Cover photograph: © Adrian Albritton/www.platimages.com

10   9   8   7   6   5   4   3   2   1

Manufactured in the United States of America

For information regarding special discounts for bulk purchases, please contact Simon & Schuster Special Sales at 1-866-506-1949 or business@simonandschuster.com

The Simon & Schuster Speakers Bureau can bring authors to your live event. For more information or to book an event, contact the Simon & Schuster Speakers Bureau at 1-866-248-3049 or visit our website at www.simonspeakers.com.

To all who have made it last forever in their relationships and those who might need help in making it last forever

ACKNOWLEDGMENTS

I want to thank all the fans who have been supportive of me through the course of my entertainment career. I really appreciate the love and support and I will never take it for granted.

INTRODUCTION

Relationships, by nature, are not easy. In fact, they are about as difficult to maintain as anything in the world. You know why? Because we are all humans, and with that comes a lot of emotions that influence how we think, what we do, how we react.

Those things determine how we function in a relationship.

And that leads us to what this book is about: determining if you have the right mate in your life and how to maintain or restart the excitement that brought you together in the first place.

For the last several years, I have spoken to thousands and thousands of listeners who called in to my nationally syndicated radio show, "The Sweat Hotel."

Reaching 1.4 million people a night through the airways means we span the country, and discover that relationship issues have no boundaries.

It does not matter where you live, how old you are, what your profession, your Zodiac sign, your sex, your religion, how much hair you have, what your complexion is, what your education background, the color of your eyes, if you have dandruff or not…We all have them. Seriously.

We have discussed every imaginable scenario and situation; and some neither you nor I could possibly have expected. We have found solutions more times than not, grown as people, comforted each other and generally learned a lot about ourselves—and how to be better mates in relationships.

It is not an exact science. In fact, it is not a science at all. This relationship thing very much is an emotionally charged, reaction-based dilemma that cannot be solved, only managed.

This book is called *Make It Last Forever*, like the hit song I recorded that became a national anthem for relationships around the world. The idea is to provide insight, tips, messages, ideas, hints, remedies...anything that will help you find the right mate for you and/or sustain your relationship. And that's what we do here. But here's the rub: This is no gimmick. This is not superficial advice. This is keeping it real at its realest.

And the reality is that some scenarios you will relate to and learn from, or at least see things from a different perspective. In other cases, you might be shocked someone has ever gone through particular scenarios or needed an outside source to consult. That's the enormity of it all: Everyone's experiences are different. But we all share a common bond: Our experiences shape our thinking, reactions and even our emotions—optimism, pessimism, hope, hopelessness—about love and relationships.

I can hear some of you whispering now: Why has *he* written this book? What makes *him* qualified? Legitimate questions. The answer is multi-fold: For one, I have experienced just about all aspects of relationships. I have had girlfriends, been married, been divorced, cheated on women, been cheated on by women, been in love when it really wasn't love, and been in love when it was true love. That spectrum of experience affords me an insight that has instilled a level-headed perspective.

Also, for the last several years, as I mentioned, I have spoken to thousands of people about relationships for three hours a night—probably more than anyone in the country. My radio show has been a virtual and figurative couch for countless listeners who have discussed their concerns with me. That incredibly deep well is the inspiration for the book—I know for a fact there are millions of people seeking direction in their relationships and lives.

Lastly, I have made my career on relationships. My music has touched people, inspired people and, I'm told, has even accounted for some babies. So, it is an area that is important to me. Relationships are really the foundation of our existence. They are what make us go—or not go. When we are in good, healthy relationships, we go about our daily lives in such a euphoric state that it can make haters hate because they do not have what we have.

At the same time, when our relationships are floundering, we feel less than what we should. Our mood is noticeably different, sour even, and we seem to expect less out of life.

That's why it is important that we establish strong, healthy relationships and/or build on relationships we already have.

Make It Last Forever is designed to help you do that very thing. We will examine many different obstacles that must be overcome, dispositions that have to be taken, adjustments that have to be made that will enhance your relationships—and we will keep it real and have fun throughout the entire journey.

CHAPTER ONE
SOMETHING JUST AIN'T RIGHT

One of the common issues I have come across is people in relationships when they should not be in a relationship. These people carry baggage so large that they would have to pay extra if they tried to check it at the airport. And yet they wonder why every relationship they have goes South.

The bottom line is this: Sometimes we simply are not ready to be in a relationship. We have to ask ourselves if we are good with whom we are at a particular moment—and then give an honest answer, which is not always easy because one of the most difficult things to do is to admit flaws in ourselves.

Are you comfortable with where you are in your life, confident that you can interact with someone without holding on to past drama? Lots of us say we are, when, in reality, we are far from that.

If a past dishonest boyfriend impacts how you view the next man in your life, then maybe you should try to figure out how to get beyond that pain before embarking on a new relationship. You think? And you know why? Because that new guy did not disappoint you and has not earned your wrath. Eventually he will say to himself: "Something just ain't right" about you when you question him about something based on your last boyfriend's behavior.

If the pain or devastation of a previous relationship—especially a recently defunct relationship—lingers within you, it is not the best time to welcome someone else into your life.

I have more than once used one woman to get past the previous woman. It was not intentional. It was natural. When you're upset or disappointed by someone, the hardest thing to do is sit around and mope about it. That's not me. I've got to keep it moving. And having that mentality, I have gotten with women I realized were not right for me, but they were there to help cushion the blow of the women before them.

Here's a classic example: When I was working on my first album, I was crazy about this woman. We were kicking it and it was all good. At some point, she visited Atlanta for her college homecoming weekend. Cool, right? Well, the entire time she was there, I could not reach her—and she didn't call me. My thought was, "Something ain't right about this."

Finally, I hear from her. And when I do, she says she's going to stay an extra few days in Atlanta. And I'm like, wow. So I started writing this song, "Something Just Ain't Right." The song was inspired by this woman who switched up on me when she went to her college homecoming.

Here are the lyrics:

Tossin', turnin', girl
I just can't sleep at night
Ooh, you've been cheating on me
Tell me it's a lie, huh

I called you home
And the phone just keeps on ringing
Ooh, baby, what do you think I am
All I wanna do is be your man

I can't sleep at night
For fear someone holdin' you tight
Make you believe you are mine
And it will be ours till the end of time

Something, something, something, something just ain't right
It just ain't right
Something, something, something, something just ain't right

Ooh, you make me feel
So good, so good inside
And the thought of another man holdin' you tight
It makes me wanna cry (Makes me want to cry)

Don't blame me if I get suspicious, baby
When you're not at home (Not at home)
You just had to look so good
Any man would want to make you his own

You, you are mine
And I, I am yours
Tell me, tell me, baby
Is it me that you adore, now tell me

Something, something, something, something just ain't right
It just ain't right
Something, something, something, something just ain't right

I did not tell our exact story, but she inspired the story by her behavior. So, finally, when she returned to New York, she said everything was okay, but I knew better. She had a girlfriend that was with her in Atlanta and I was cool with her. So, I asked her friend what was up. She said, "Keith, you're a nice guy, but your girl was with another man."

I knew it. I felt it. But she confirmed it for me. So I manned up and dealt with it. She hung around with me until I finished the album. But once I finished it, I was finished with her.

The point of that story is that after that, the next person I dealt with was dealing with the residuals of what I recently endured. She wasn't really dealing with me. And I wasn't really dealing with her. I was trying to get past that episode and I used that woman to help further my cause. It was not fair to her, but it still happened. I was younger back then and I see it now all the time. But jumping into a relationship right after one suddenly ends should not happen.

Work on getting *yourself* right first. Doesn't that make sense? Forget about anyone else. If you are not right, things that normally may not irritate you will bother you to no end. When you're not right, your patience level diminishes. When you're not right, you smile less and frown more, making it an unpleasant environment. How can you be a positive asset to someone else when you have your own issues to overcome?

That is extremely hard to do. When we are free of past baggage or issues, we free ourselves to embrace something new and good. Our minds and hearts are open to new experiences and growth.

When we hang on to past pain and disappointment, we shut down. We look for the next disaster around the corner. We anticipate disappointment. We wait for drama. We limit our growth.

The way to be fair in a relationship is to be beyond that. That will allow you to give the benefit of the doubt in questionable situations. Everyone should have that advantage until he/she ruins it. This is different from being foolish. I would never condone being foolish or to ignore the obvious. Do not look past something right in your face; that's the worst thing you can do. But if feelings creep to the surface because a situation might be similar to something bad you experienced, you must be in a frame of mind to let it play out without being judgmental and jumping to dramatic conclusions.

It also would be wise to not jump into a relationship when you are still holding intense feelings for your last boyfriend. If you are still in love with one man, you're probably not ready for another relationship until you get over him.

So many callers over the years have talked about trying to get over one guy by dating another guy. My answer is always the same: You're not being fair to the new man when you are with him but wishing you were with someone else.

Most times, we can overcome or see a situation better if we do one basic thing: Put ourselves in the other person's position. If we do that, we would understand that it would be totally unfair to use one person to get over another.

Sometimes we are so eager to get past our pain and disappointment that we jump right into the next opportunity, thinking that being involved with someone will push us beyond the past. Seldom does that ever work.

And think about it: Would you like to be that "rebound" person, thinking you have met someone with the potential to be good for you, but all the while, you are there simply to fill a void left by someone else? That would be totally unfair and you'd feel cheap.

One of the things we have to stop doing to each other is using each other.

"That didn't work out, so I'll deal with him until I get back with my old boyfriend or get over him."

Again, totally unfair—and you wouldn't want it to happen to you.

It boils down to being fair over being selfish. It is selfish behavior to get from someone what you are not willing to offer, or to use someone to get back on your emotional feet, when you know you have no true feelings for that person.

So where does that leave us?

Alone.

And there is nothing wrong with that. In fact, it is probably the best place to be after a relationship ends. Alone time is when we can make assessments about who we are as a person and who we were in that relationship. It is much more difficult to do if you are too quickly trying to move on to the next partner.

The harsh reality is that unless you have taken the time to understand your role in the failure of the relationship—and have come to some agreement on how to bring change to yourself—then you are not ready to embark on a new relationship.

Jumping right to the next person would be the equivalent of carrying toxins with you, meaning you are bound to poison the next relationship. Toxins in your body are like a virus—they fester in you, spread and eventually do destruction, if not treated. It is the same way with relationships.

If you don't treat the toxins of a bad relationship, the virus grows and festers to the point where it shows itself in many ways that could hurt your new relationship.

How? Well, that depends on what happened in the previous relationship. But almost always trust issues come to the forefront. You don't trust that the relationship will flourish. You don't trust that the person in the relationship will do right by you. You don't trust yourself to embrace happiness.

That's a lot of mistrust to overcome. When it's that heavy, it's best to work on you before pairing up with someone else.

KEITH'S KEY: There has been more than one time when I used one woman to get over the previous woman. I'm not proud of it, but it happened. I wasn't ready for a new relationship, and sure enough the next one that I jumped into so quickly failed. Badly.

Looking back on it now, it is all so clear to me. When there was a bad or sudden breakup, it was during those times that I wanted to psychologically get past the relationship quickly, and the natural thing to me was to find the next woman to heal my wounds, so to speak.

And it would work for a while. I would feel like, "Okay, I'm moving on," as if I were getting the first woman out of my system. But I was actually moving backward or, at best, running in place. I was not advancing my life because, unfortunately, the next person was not the right person. She was merely the convenient person.

I feel bad about those cases when I did that. Truth be told, I was not giving that second woman a legitimate chance since I was not my real self.

But here's the very actual part: There was probably no right person for me at that time. The best thing for me to do was to be by myself, assess my role in the failure of the relationship and then make the necessary changes to not repeat them next time when I got involved with someone. That would have been the fair thing to do for the next woman in my life—and for myself.

CHAPTER TWO
OPPOSITES ATTRACT...FOR A WHILE

There is this overused expression that makes sense, in one way, but makes absolutely no sense in another: opposites attract.

For the longest, I believed wholeheartedly in it. It seemed to make sense. If I was this way, I needed a woman who was not like me for us to be harmonious.

The philosophy was that we would somehow balance each other out. I also believed that two people with the same personalities and idiosyncrasies would be too similar, which would ultimately lead to chaos and conflict.

Like many people, I have learned the hard way that opposite personalities together do not make for the best relationship. In the long run, those differences are too different and create an insurmountable bridge to gap.

It always starts out the same, though. We are captivated by the differences in the other person. In one of my cases, this woman was slightly more outgoing than me. I'm a laid-back kind of guy. I usually like to observe and kick back. Well, this particular woman was not like that. She was assertive and the life of the party.

I liked it...at first. It showed her confidence and her zest for life. She was fun and exciting to be around. Her energy lifted my spirits and gave me energy. But as time wore on, those same "qualities" I enjoyed about her began to irritate me. She was "on" all the time, meaning she did not consider laying back and relaxing. That was boring to her. What I perceived as cute in the beginning gradually began to turn ugly. The energy that captured my attention wore me down. Her assertiveness got on my nerves.

Meanwhile, my laid-back nature began to bother her. In short, we began to clash.

Suddenly, small disagreements would pop up. Nothing big...at first. But they were enough to irritate each other or ruin an evening. Eventually, the arguments got bigger and bigger and turned into full-blown arguments.

The worst thing about it was that we both acknowledged the clashes of personalities, but we continued to try to make it work. That was a bad move. The more we irritated each other, the more we argued and the more we argued, the more miserable we were together.

Staying in it resulted in an ugly breakup, with name-calling and bad feelings.

You would think that would have clued me in on dating women who did not have common personalities. But it didn't.

There was the woman who was a homebody. She didn't desire to go many places. It was great at first. She wasn't concerned about being seen with me in public. She was settled and calm. She slowed me down some. But we lived in Atlanta, where there was so much to do, so much to see. To stay in all the time did not make much sense to me.

Finally, I asserted myself and insisted we get out and embrace some of what there was to experience in the city. Well, that was a waste of time. She didn't want to be there, and she looked and acted like it.

Basically, she pouted the entire time. As far as I was concerned, she did not even try to make the most of the night. She would sit there, bored and disinterested. Of course, that made the night horrible for me as well. She was the extreme opposite of the other woman, but still not compatible with me.

And that's what all the drama is about when it comes to unsuccessful relationships—or simply keeping the energy and excitement in the relationship you have. It's all about compatibility, selecting the right mate.

What are the criteria we set when choosing a mate? Is it because you think the guy is cute or handsome that you should be with him? Are you captured by his gift of gab, the things he says to you that make you feel good? Is it his job or status in the community? Is it how tall he is? Is it his teeth? Is it the car he drives? The house he lives in?

Don't laugh. I have heard all these reasons and more for women wanting to be involved with a man in a relationship. And therein lies the problem. Our choices.

Not only do opposites not work in many cases, but we are bound for similar disappointment when we make mate selections based on superficial ideals. Superficial things include someone's possessions or looks—anything that does not speak to the kind of *person* he or she is.

We all like nice things and are attracted to particular physical attributes of someone. But if that is what we base our relationship decision on—no matter how rude he or she might be or dishonest or unreliable or plain ole mean—then we set ourselves up for drama that could be avoided with selecting the right person for the right reasons.

That leads us to the natural question: What are the right reasons to select a mate?

In my years as an entertainer traveling the world and as a talk radio show host, I have heard and/or experienced, in one way or another, countless cases of people getting involved in relationships for reasons that did not add up.

Reasons that make sense to me are many. You should not select a mate based on a single attribute. It should be more about a package that could bring you comfort and fulfillment in a number of areas:

RESPECTABILITY. The person you're interested in should command respect because of the kind of person he is and because of the respect he gives. If someone is highly respected, it speaks to his character. And when it comes to you, he should be especially respectful in the way he communicates with you; the language he uses; how he receives your thoughts; how he presents himself around you. At the same time, you must command respect from everyone. If you are aggressive toward a man, you can bet his level of respect for you will instantly diminish because you've put yourself out there. His aggression will top yours, as he identifies your weakness or overt interest. That's not to say you should play games or not let your feelings be known; it's all in how it is done. Throwing yourself at someone you hardly know is not the way to earn his respect. Also, if the use of profanity is something you are uncomfortable with, you have to let that be known by the language you use. As a woman, you should stand at the door and let the man know you expect him to open it for you. That's commanding respect. The same at the car door or just walking down the street. He should not walk in front of you and he should walk on the outside, closest to the street. The sad thing is that many times you might have to let the person know that's what you expect, although it should be as natural to man as drinking water to open the door for a woman, etc.

THOUGHTFULNESS. Someone you're interested in and who has interest in you should show that he has an unselfish nature, that he considers you and your feelings, what you would like in the things that he does daily. For example, if you talk to him about how tired you are after work, it should occur to him to either offer to prepare dinner for you or to take you out to dinner. That's a thoughtful act that shows he cares, as that's pretty much what thoughtfulness is. It's caring enough to do an act that shows you care. It is not about purchasing fancy jewelry or taking luxurious trips. Those things are wonderful, but should come only as a natural part of the growth of the relationship over time. Thoughtfulness is making time to say "have a nice day" in the morning. With technology and the incessant love for text-messaging, being thoughtful is very easy and unobtrusive. A thoughtful text message can bring a smile and show that you care. However, this is in no way endorsing a relationship built on text-messaging. When someone over-loads you with text-messages and calls you less, that's a sign of something wrong. A properly timed text message, on occasion, lends the kind of thoughtfulness that lets you know the person wants to be in touch with you and wants you to be in tune with him.

AMBITION. We all should desire someone who has goals in their professional and personal life, as they offer a glimpse into what the future might be like. The tough economy has put many people in difficult positions as it relates to jobs, but that is no excuse for someone to not be up every day pounding the pavement, seeking work. If someone does not work or hardly works and does not try hard to reverse their situation, that tells you something—and it's not good. It speaks to laziness or a lack of fire…something that does not promote a commitment to succeed. And in short, who wants to be with a loser? Success should not be measured in how much money someone makes. It should be measured in someone's ability to earn a living, to provide for himself and/or family, his diligence about his job, and how well he does his job. Those are the elements of ambition, and if someone is ambitious in his job, it shows he has drive that he can use to be successful in relationships.

That's how you make a decision on whether or not you are compatible with someone. Concrete traits that speak to who the person is, his/her foundation. Then you can add the other characteristics or even superficial things like looks, hair, skin complexion, etc.

The thinking is this: when someone has the foundation, he has a stable base from which to build. It does not matter if the man is drop-dead gorgeous or has money or has a nice car if he does not know how to treat you, if he's not respectable, if he's not thoughtful, or if he's lazy.

Think about it this way: Find a nice box with a beautiful wrapping on the outside of it. Looks wonderful. Then, when you approach the box, you pick it up and discover that it is light. Empty.

Eye candy is good for a while, but it can often turn rotten. So it is best to find that person who is attractive to you and has the elements of character that at least give you the impression that he is of substance.

CHAPTER THREE

ROMANCE IS EASIER THAN YOU THINK

The essence of any good relationship is the romance put into it—from both sides. But don't trip: it's not about buying big diamond rings or new cars, although no one would reject that kind of generosity.

It's really about little things, things that show you care, that show you're in tune with your mate's personality and needs. As men, we quickly fall back in the "I'm not a mind-reader" position when we do not provide what a woman needs. We claim they have not told us, so how can we know?

Well, here's the thing: You don't have to be a mind-reader to be connected to your partner. All you have to do is pay attention. That's so important, I'll write it again: All you have to do is pay attention.

Paying attention gets you *everywhere*. You pay attention and you know what makes your mate tick, what makes him excited, what inspires him, what is important to him.

It could not be simpler than that. If you listen closely enough, your mate will tell you what he desires or needs in his communication to you. It likely will not be something blatant or direct. It will require you to pay attention.

For example, if he mentions an interest in golf, getting him a golf lesson is a thoughtful idea, something that would make him feel like you are connected to him, which promotes good feelings, which promotes romance. It's all connected.

I know of a case where a guy really liked a woman, but did not think it was appropriate to shower her with expensive gifts. So, instead, he sent her a package with items he knew she liked that would show he was connected to her: a book with quotes by notable people because she was big on wise quotations; a DVD he believed she would like because she indicated she liked movies; a seashell because she loved the ocean; a twenty-dollar gift card to Starbucks because she often started her day with a cup of java; a CD of romantic music they had shared.

The woman found the gesture thoughtful and romantic. In every case, he showed that he listened to her, paid attention to her likes, and was connected to her. Romantic.

The other item in that package was a letter. He had done something that, in this day of technological advances, is a lost art. Who writes letters anymore, other than inmates? E-mails, yes. Text messages, definitely. But someone taking the time and thought to sit down and put pen to paper is about as popular as the typewriter, which actually is sad.

It takes effort and caring to write someone a thoughtful letter, put a stamp on an envelope, and mail it. To make that effort shows more than a passing interest. It shows you care.

And to lace it with expressions of how you feel about the recipient takes the romance to another level. It is worth the effort. Trust me.

All that is cool, but it takes something many people do not have to even grasp the concept of being romantic or doing for others. And that trait is unselfishness.

Most people are centered on getting *their* needs fulfilled. They want to feel special, to have someone do for them. It's actually a very natural thing. But it takes being unselfish to do for others. You must understand: If you're involved with a righteous person, your kind, thoughtful, romantic acts will inspire them to be kind, thoughtful and romantic to you.

But how do you get to be unselfish? That's the million-dollar question. If it is not in your nature to want to please, how do you make it part of your personality?

Well, the first thing is to *want* to be selfless. To be romantic is to be focused on someone else, which, for some people, is a very difficult thing to do. But if you can step outside of yourself and center your thoughts on that person in your life, you will be able to adjust your focus on being a pleaser.

The thing is, most people are takers. They will take whatever comes their way that they want to accept. And that wouldn't be a problem if you were also a pleaser. Usually, though, you are either a taker or a pleaser, not both.

I believe it is better to be a pleaser because that means you are unselfish and, therefore, ultimately you treat that person in your life with care and respect, which will inspire the same out of him toward you. That's how it works.

So, be the romantic in your relationship. Be unselfish. Connect with your mate. Listen to what he/she says. Then act on those things you learn from paying attention. It's romantic—and it will spark a romantic nature in the one you love.

Why is all this important? Because in a relationship, it is easy to get bored, easy to get settled and complacent. If you really care about your mate and want to return to (or initiate) more excitement and energy into the relationship, arguing or complaining about it is not the way to go.

The idea should be to counter concerns with romance. There are plenty of elements to being romantic:

❤ I've already mentioned paying attention, being in tune to what your partner's interests or desires are.

❤ Candles. Scented candles create a sensual mood through the flickering light they provide to the wonderful aromas they spread. Setting a mood for romance means inspiring relaxation and ease. Turning down the lights and having candles create a dark but peaceful room, making for a romantic scene. Studies have indicated particular scents from candles generate frisky feelings in people. For instance, lavender and jasmine are ideal for making one relax and release muscle tension that builds up throughout the course of a day. Remember what Teddy Pendergrass sang: "Just turn out the lights… and light a candle."

❤ Music. Hey, I should really know about this, right? Sometimes, the lyrics and music set a mood of romance and closeness. I have heard from many who said they have made babies to my music, which is the ultimate compliment. You create love songs to make an impact on people, to bring them together so they can enjoy each other in an open and relaxed way. That's what music does. So, when seeking romance, find the right music, the music that speaks to how you're feeling and how you want your partner to feel. I love hip-hop music as much as the next person, but for romance, you should choose something with soothing tones and alluring lyrics that help promote intimacy.

♥ Lingerie. That always works. Give him a sultry glimpse at what you have to offer and you can bet romance will ensue. That's a very critical piece. So many women fall into a rut and believe because the man is there, he should automatically be attracted to her. The reality is that he needs to look at someone sexy to be sexual toward her. Going to bed in flannel pajamas or big T-shirts do not promote him wanting to be romantic with you. I understand sometimes you just don't feel like the teddy or the slinky lingerie. But that's where the sacrifice comes in to keep him desiring you.

Also, there are many women who are so mindful of how their hair must look tomorrow that they are not interested in keeping it sexy for their man that night, which is another problem. Going to bed looking like raggedy is not the way to seduce your man. Of course, no one feels like looking like a sexpot every night. But if you want your man's attention, it is important to make him see you in all your sexiness. At the least you should remove the hair wrap until after you and your man have completed the romantic evening.

Does it go both ways? Of course. A man should not go to bed looking like he's about to go play ball and expect that to make his woman feel all warm inside. He has to find the silk boxers or snugly fit tank top—whatever it is his mate likes—and be about it.

In the end, this really is about complacency, or not being complacent. The biggest killer of romance is getting so comfortable with your mate that you believe you don't have to do anything anymore. Not true. Showing up is not good enough, even if neither party says anything about it.

You can bet a dollar to a donut that there is someone else out there admiring your partner and giving him/her the attention that you are not. And I don't care how honest or innocent someone is, if someone gives him something you are not giving him—compliments and attention in particular—there is the very real potential of your mate embracing that new person.

And you know why he or she would? Because people feed off feeling good about themselves. Think about yourself: Don't you need to know that you look good? Don't you want someone to acknowledge that you are taking care of yourself? Don't you want to feel like the effort you put into looking good is appreciated?

Well, if you need that for yourself, you can bet your man or woman needs it, too. And it doesn't matter how long you all have been together. It doesn't matter if your mate doesn't seem to get much out of you saying, "You look good." As Nike says, just do it.

It may not seem to matter, but it does. And it shows that—despite the length of time you have been together—that you really care and that you do not take her/him for granted.

Which leads me to another important point. There have been studies done that identify the top reasons the romance in a relationship fails and one mate will step out on the other mate with someone else. And guess what the No. 1 reason is for infidelity?

It is the feeling of being taken for granted. And that comes totally with complacency. When you become really familiar with your mate, there is a natural tendency to relax and even foster a bit of indifference. That's what we have to guard against because you can rest assured that your mate feels the slippage in compliments and attention.

Sometimes it is not even about conscious slights. Sometimes it's just about life. You get into a routine that plays itself out day after day. You discuss what the kids did in school and what household responsibilities need to be handled, grocery shopping, paying bills and other necessary things. You talk about everything except you or your needs or even the relationship in general. Before the kids came along, or the extremely demanding job, you often relaxed and discussed your plans as a couple, how wonderful it was to connect, future trips—all sorts of conversations that brought you closer together.

Then, over time, you achieve some of the things you talked about, but the weight of life gets heavy. And along the way, a woman in particular, can feel like an afterthought to her man who no longer compliments her or has meaningful conversations with her. So, when she's feeling neglected, she's most vulnerable to find a coworker's or acquaintance's advances quite alluring and tempting, seductive.

The same thing applies for a man. If his woman fails over a period of time to provide intimacy or some sort of emotional connection, he will be susceptible to the attention another woman might pay him.

KEITH'S KEY: What it all comes down to is this: Maintaining romance in the relationship is critical. And you cannot do it by jumping in bed, saying, "I'm ready." There should be a seduction—candles, music, alluring attire—involved that starts with being attentive to your mate's needs and listening and hearing when he/she expresses the desires of their heart. Fight off complacency by reinforcing your connection to your partner. Talk to him/her about them and not just about the issues of the day. Compliment each other and be conscious of creating emotional satisfaction. Looking outside the relationship will not come into play because inside the relationship is someone who brings comfort, joy, attention and respect.

CHAPTER FOUR

NEW TECHNOLOGY/OLD TRICKS: TRUST IS ABOUT TRUSTING

'm sometimes amazed at how many people still do not understand that laptops and cell phones are virtually tracking devices. And if you are up to no good in your relationship, those really cool items can be bring you a lot of heat.

There have been countless callers into the "Sweat Hotel" who have told stories of reading e-mails or text messages of their loved ones that damaged their relationships.

Through reading their e-mails and/or text messages, they learned about dates with other people, interest in other people, or flat-out steamy affairs.

The lesson in this is simple: If you look, you will find something. And even the most innocent thing can be misinterpreted to be the worst thing.

In the days before personal computers and high-tech cell phones, the snooping spouse would take place via men going through women's purses or ladies rifling through pants pockets or checking the collars of shirts for lipstick or makeup smudges.

Whether going through someone's e-mails, phone, her purse, or his pockets, it's wrong. Period. This is a problem that speaks to one thing: lack of trust.

Lack of trust is the No. 1 killer of relationships. It infests a relationship, poisons it, weakens it and ultimately destroys it. Every time. To make a relationship last forever the trust issues have to be overcome.

The first thing that must be done is to trust yourself to trust. Do you get that? You have to have trust in yourself that it's okay to let go of the inhibitions, doubts, and speculation. Trusting yourself allows you to give the person in your life the benefit of the doubt. You're able to deal with him or her on their own merits, not the behavior of the past.

And if you get there, then you will not feel the need to sneak through someone's e-mails or phone or belongings. That's an invasion of privacy that simply should not happen. But it's hard to fight. I am guilty of going through a woman's phone.

I'm not proud to admit it, but I was at a place where I did not understand, or even care, about invading her privacy. I wanted confirmation of what I was feeling. That's the crazy part about it: You don't search to *not* find something; you search because you feel something and you want to confirm your feelings, even if what you find will hurt your feelings.

So, when you think about it that way, it's a pretty sick thing to do. Going through people's personal property or e-mails, etc., should make you feel bad, if you have a conscience. And we shouldn't do anything that makes us feel bad.

The way to confront our questions is to confront our mate—not disrespect his/her space. Confronting calmly and with respect does two things: It should make your partner feel comfortable and not get on the defensive; and it lets him/her know you are not making a judgment, that you are trusting that he will be honest. That's a strong position to begin an important conversation.

That conversation—and any conversation—has to be candid and true. The real, foolproof way to build trust is to be about your word. If you are impeccable with your word—meaning you mean what you say and you do what you say you will do—it gives your mate reason to trust that you are reliable.

And that is not just about the big things, either. It's especially about the little things, like calling when you say you will call. Believe it or not, your mate hangs on to what you say, so it's really important to do what you say you will.

Many times, something beyond our control impacts us keeping our word. You might plan on being at her house at seven o'clock. But perhaps there was a last-minute meeting at work that threw you off—or traffic. In those cases, a phone call (or even a text in these days of phone overuse) would be appropriate. It is not right to show up late without any regard for the person waiting on you. That's not being henpecked or weak. It's being *right*.

One time, I was more than an hour late picking up this nice woman for a date. I was so caught up in returning phone calls and handling business that I didn't let her know I would be so late. When I got there, she had this apparent attitude. I finally asked her what the problem was.

"You're an hour late, Keith," she said.

At the time, I didn't get it. I was there, she was ready, and it was time to go on and have a good time. But the reality was that because I did not call her, followed by not understanding why she was so upset, we didn't have a nice evening. I could have prevented that bad experience twice: once, by calling her to let her know I was behind time and, twice, by apologizing when I did get there.

That's the responsible thing to do, something that will build trust within your partner. Some people might consider that petty. I consider it being mature and respectful.

There's another way to destroy trust, though. And that's by your behavior. I've been cheated on, and I knew it. You know how I knew? Because the woman would never answer her cell phone around me. She would keep it at her side every second of the day, even taking it to the bathroom. She would have it on vibrate all the time. And she would always find time to send text messages.

If those are not signs of someone with something else going on, I don't know what would be. I didn't have to go searching for anything with her— her behavior told the entire story.

In an ideal world, you should be able to leave your e-mail account open without fear of your mate going in and reading your stuff. But we're hardly living in an ideal world. So, you log out of your e-mail every time you step away from it, even if there is nothing there to see because you understand anything can be determined to be improper. It's a tough place to be.

When you can see your mate's phone sitting by itself or his/her e-mail open and do not go into it, that's a huge sign of trust. Your mate would appreciate it and you would feel really proud of yourself for resisting the urge. But that's what has to happen. That's not to say to be stupid and blind to the obvious. But it is saying that we have to give the benefit of the doubt and not make it a common practice to search for the smoking gun, so to speak, that could blow up the relationship.

KEITH'S KEY: Use the wonders of the advanced technology to *enhance* your relationship, not to cause drama in the one you're in. Facebook has been considered a top destroyer of relationships in recent years because so many people go on it to find others they might be interested in. And, inevitably, your partner finds out and nothing good comes from that.

Same with e-mails and text messaging. Instead of pursuing others, how about sending a nice text message to your mate during the course of the day to reassure him/her about how you feel. Something simple works just fine: "Just letting you know I'm thinking of you, baby." You'd be shocked at how much joy that kind of communication provides amid a hectic workday.

I mentioned writing a letter earlier, the dying art. Well, if you just don't have the time to put pen to paper, put fingers to keys and send a surprising e-mail to your lover, expressing how you feel about him/her or how pleased you were about something you did together. These kinds of gestures show that you are not taking that person for granted and, significantly, they build trust.

Think about it: Aren't you prone to feeling better about your mate when you are consistently reminded by him that you matter, that he's thinking of you, that he's looking forward to being with you? Again, it's the little things that add up to something really big that adds peace and trust.

CHAPTER FIVE

BE A PLEASER...AND KEEP PLEASING

There's a saying that is simple but very profound: You should start the way you plan to finish. In a relationship, that definitely applies in a number of areas, including, and especially, the bedroom. That's keeping it real, you know?

Problems in the bedroom create a serious mess in a relationship. And it usually happens from one or two reasons:

❤ You connect with someone you really like but he does not make you see stars when making love. And you *like* to see stars. Eventually, not physically pleasing you becomes a problem. A *real* problem.

❤ He pleases you at the start, but then gets complacent and the sex becomes an afterthought. You want it, but he doesn't provide it. Or when he provides it, it's not what it used to be.

Not good, in both cases. I have heard too many times about women who married men for the right reasons, but not *all* the right reasons. If having good, exciting sex is important to you, then you should make sure that's what your mate gives you.

Makes sense, right? I mean, if you like to dress up as Wonder Woman and swing from a chandelier, if that's what turns you on, then you should be with someone who likes to see you swing from a chandelier dressed as Wonder Woman. That's just how it should go if that is important to you.

I'll tell anybody: If you put sex in a relationship as something not very important, although you *really* like it, then you're setting yourself up for drama. I don't care how nice the guy is or how much of a provider he is and how much your friends like him and how well he treats you. If you need the physical, sexual satisfaction that comes with sex and he's not giving it to you, there will be a time when you will crave it so badly that you will think about getting it outside your relationship, you will fantasize about it, and when the time comes, you will get it.

That's a hard truth. Trust me, I know. I have encountered and been propositioned by dozens and dozens of women who have stepped to me even though they were married or in a relationship. And many times, when I asked them why they were coming at me when they had a man, their response would be, "He's not putting it down."

Some women, let's be honest here, will put themselves in that position just because that's what they want to do, no matter how the man is treating them at home. That's being real. But most of the women I'm referring to were good, wholesome women whose bodies were not being taken care of by their men.

The worst part of it is that some of them told me their men *never* really pleased them in bed. They appreciated the way the men looked, their personalities and their success…all important stuff in being with someone. They said they figured the sex would get better over time. Well, they figured wrong.

There's this one woman I know. She's a professional woman who is beautiful and smart and as grounded as they come. Well, she got married to a guy she considered right out of her dreams: tall, handsome, athletic. He treated her nicely and they looked great together as a couple. Her friends were envious because she was happy and she had a man who looked the part.

During their dating days, he did not please her in bed. They both lived with their parents, so she figured it was merely a byproduct of them doing it in the car or rushing while no one was home…anything other than the fact that he was not a good lover.

So, of course, she ignored her private concerns, and married the guy. And do you know that it took the *honeymoon* for her to realize she was in trouble? Finally, they were husband and wife; she had the man of her dreams. They did not have to sneak around for sex or rush through it. They were married and on their honeymoon, the most romantic time they would ever have together.

But, instead of knocking her boots, causing her body to tremble and ache in that way only good lovemaking can produce, she got nothing. When I say nothing, I mean nothing.

They were in Orlando at a resort. She's the kind of woman who sets up romance with ease. The candles were burning. She was in a beautiful negligee. Her body was hot from anticipation of steamy, passionate sex with her new husband. It was time for her concerns about sex in her married life to be put to rest. Rather, on the first night of their honeymoon, the husband could not sustain an erection. So this new bride who was craving mind-blowing sex got no sex at all.

The next day, they went to Disney in 100-degree heat and only lasted an hour; it was unbearably hot. Back in the room, the couple went to sleep. She was devastated.

That night, she initiated sex and they did have it. But it was just as bland and unexciting as always. They completed the honeymoon in less-than-extraordinary fashion and returned home.

When the new bride—less than two weeks after she was married—got back to her job, she used her downtime to write a short fantasy about meeting a married man who would please her sexually over and over again. She wanted it, *needed* it so badly in her life, that she wrote about it. And guess what happened. She eventually found that married man—it was not me, by the way—who gave her the physical, sexual pleasure her body had craved for so long.

That's how important sex is in a relationship: a wonderful woman who was not getting it resorted to something she never thought she would do to get it. She is not proud of her actions—and they have long since been divorced—but her actions and frustrations illustrate how critical something many would consider trivial actually is anything but trivial. It's critical.

That example might be an extreme case, but there are so many where the woman was not pleased at the start of the relationship, but she stayed in it because she hoped it would get better. The reality is that hope is not going to get you to feel the way you need to feel.

And it goes both ways, too. I have heard from countless men who cannot believe that the women they had mad, crazy, hot sex with suddenly became unexciting and disinterested in sex.

Sometimes, especially with career women with children, the burden of work, raising kids, and life itself drains them so much that the husbands and mates are the ones who are left out of the mix. The women prioritize that other things matter more and by the time they go to bed, they are hardly interested in expending the energy to do all the things that turned their men out in the first place.

He's looking for a little oral love, and she's so worn out from the day's activities that she's just not interested. He wants her in a different position; she wants to lie on her back, basically saying, "Okay, if you've got to do this, go ahead and get it over."

And he's like, "Are you serious?" And just like, with the displeased, unful-filled woman, the man begins to think about venturing off to an old lover who pleased him, or seeking someone new—anything that will fulfill his unfulfilled sexual craving.

Basically, that's how it happens. I know, I know. Yes, there are some men AND women—let's not put it all on the men—who will go out and seek other sex partners just because they are promiscuous and seek variety. But this isn't about them. This is about keeping your partner.

And the best way to do that is to never get complacent. That's what it comes down to, doesn't it? It's either that, or you put yourself in a bad position by getting with someone who you knew could not please you.

If you are with someone who does not please you to the point where you are thinking about or have already stepped out on him, then it's obvious what should happen. You shouldn't be with that person. It is unfair to your mate and, really, unfair to you. You should have what you desire and should seek it all within one person.

That's really the problem in most cases where a tired love life is concerned. You know the person did not please you, and yet, you try to convince your-self that it will come or that it does not matter that much. But you've only tried to fool yourself. And you do not fool yourself for long.

All this could have been avoided long ago. How? By telling your partner exactly what you wanted when you realized you were not getting all you desired. It's that simple. I have heard people say, "I didn't want to hurt his feelings." Well, you can believe that he'd rather know what you want than to think he's giving you what you like. Unless there is some physical concern, that man can work on being the lover you need, thereby eliminating your need as you get more and more frustrated to seek pleasure somewhere else.

It is not an easy conversation to have. If you have a heart, you do not want to hurt someone's feelings. At the same time, you cannot let the person think he's doing a great job—in essence, faking it—when he's not. That's misleading—and will lead you down the path of misleading your mate further in the future. So, it's best to lead him/her. You have to be delicate with the instructions. You can't blurt out. You have to ease your way into it and even offer suggestions that he considers doing what he is not doing.

"You know what?" you could begin. "I like it when you do this. How about trying *this*?"

It's worth a try to get what you need out of the person you care for.

If it turns out that your mate has told you what he/she likes and you have not given it to him/her, it's a pretty good idea that you start doing what they ask. We've already said it is hard for most people to ask for what they want in bed, for fear of hurting feelings. So, it was a big thing for him to ask for what he wants, but he did it because it was important to him.

You cannot take that lightly. As a married couple, in particular, there should be no limits to pleasing your mate. I know a guy who shocked me: He told me that his wife never performed oral sex on him. It was too preposterous to believe he was joking.

I tried not to sound nosey, but I had to know: "Have you asked for it?" I said.

"Hell, yeah, I did," he said. "But she said, 'no.'"

He and his wife of nearly twenty years battled over this issue for years. They went to a marriage counselor at their church. The assistant pastor told her it was her duty as his wife to adhere to his wishes. She refused. Her reason: She just didn't want to do it.

They went to a family counselor who again shared with his wife that she pleased her husband as a part of her wedding vows to him. She asked the husband if there were limits to what he would do to please his wife, and he told the counselor there were no limits.

When his wife was asked why she would not perform this act, she answered: "Because I think it's nasty."

Told it was a natural part of sex and an immature position, she responded, "Whatever."

And so, her husband eventually sought what he desired from someone else. They stayed together for a while, years, but the husband hardly was content. It was not everything, but it was important because not only did he not get what he desired from his wife, but her refusal also meant to him that she did not care enough to step beyond her boundaries to please her man.

What do you think happened? If you guessed that she ended up losing her husband, you are correct.

Now, in a different scenario, if you started out having lights-out sex with your partner, but it has become stale or virtually non-existent, then it is up to you to save your relationship. If you are the person who has changed, who no longer does the extra tricks or treats, who is worn out from work and the kids and just wants to get it over with…if that's you, then you have work to do.

First thing to do is to acknowledge that you have been less than you should be to your mate. No, that's not easy to do, but that's how you get started. Then make a commitment to reversing your situation. Simply put, just do it. Make the time to be a pleasing sexual partner. Do not give in to excuses.

Find the energy—through exercise, rest, or just plain will—to please your man. It would help if couples understood the value of dating the person they are involved in.

It is very easy to get into a routine that can get monotonous and boring: Work, come home, work with the kids on their homework, prepare dinner and go to bed with the idea of doing it all over again the next day.

Intimacy with the husband or wife becomes an afterthought, something that happens—if it happens—but is not a big deal. If it does not happen, well, that's fine, too. And that's a recipe for relationship disaster.

Intimacy in the bedroom with your mate cannot be a secondary thing. It has to be something that really is at the forefront of your thinking because you can believe it is at the forefront of his—whether he says something or not. And even if it does not seem like a priority to him, it should be a priority to you.

Why? Because intimacy is the backbone of any relationship. You date and flirt with each other and fantasize about being in the bed together through-out the dating period until it happens. And you do that because that's the ultimate expression of how you feel about someone. Putting it into poetic words is great, if you can do that. But articulating it physically pleases your mate more times than not and is the expression of all expressions.

Life is so demanding that it sometimes gets in the way. It wears you down, sucks the energy and enthusiasm out of you—and then there's a man there waiting to be pleased. And you're like: "I'm tired…Tomorrow—I promise."

And tomorrow never really comes. And when it does, it's not like it was back in the day, when pleasing him was everything to you. You knew going in that the right way was the *only* way to keep him/her. So you put all your energy and effort and imagination into it—and you disregarded any inhibitions you might have had because the goal was to please.

Then you get that person you want hooked—you've been all you can be, making her/him call your name and spend days at work thinking about the next encounter with you.

Down the line, after you have him/her on the hook, you get complacent and you rest on what you *used* to do, how you put it down back then. Well, truth be told, you're only as good as your last session.

But here's the wild thing about it: Sometimes, it's really not about not feeling your partner anymore. Sometimes it's about the routine of it all. There's no creativity, no passion. Not because you don't love or care about your partner. It simply gets dry. It becomes something to do to blow off some steam and then go to sleep.

That's understandable with the way life is today. But it's still not acceptable among mates. Someone has to grasp that the relationship is faltering and take a stand. And that stand is simple: Bring back the romance.

If someone does not step up and do something, you could get into a rut that is so deep you may not be able to escape. And bringing the romance back does not equate to trips to the French Riviera or Swiss Alps. It's about dating your mate.

You must find things to do together that promote closeness—movies, drinks at a lounge, bowling, dancing, picnics. And you must engage in these activities regularly.

Perhaps the hardest thing to do is to keep the zest in a relationship after it settles down. Going on a date without the kids forces you to stay out of a rut and places you in a mode of having fun and enjoying each other.

You're heard of couples having "date nights" once a month or so, which is cool. But if you can do it more often, the chances of feeling neglected or in a routine are minimized.

For instance, the occasional lunch date with your spouse, or better half, would be a way of keeping things sizzling. It would be more than lunch. It would be an effort to show how much you care, and that sometimes gets lost in dealing with the day-to-day demands of life.

KEITH'S KEY: Above all, you have to avoid the rut that many relationships fall into that cause their imminent doom. You cannot put enough emphasis on how important having consistent passion is to a relationship. If you start off being King Kong or Queen Kong in bed, you'd better make sure to keep it going throughout the relationship to please your partner because that's exactly what your partner needs and expects.

In lengthy relationships, it's hard to sustain the excitement. But the only way to keep your mate from having wandering eyes is to be conscious of it and to put in the work. When people talk of work in a relationship, that's where the work comes in—keeping it sexy and exciting. Don't be afraid of that work. Be excited about it. And be the lover your mate wants and needs.

CHAPTER SIX

PERFORMANCE VS. *PERFORMANCE*

When I am on stage, I put on a show—but I am also delivering a message. And since the majority of my fans are women, that message is one of romance and seduction. It also is important to my brothers who support me; it could help generate ideas for them to set a mood of romance with their mates.

My theme is all about mood. On my stage are leather couches that flank burning candles and a vase of roses. The lights are dim. My music promotes love and affection—or at the very least, emotion. If a fan visualized what the "Sweat Hotel" lobby looks like, we try to simulate it as much as we can on stage.

You watch my show and you see that I relate to the audience. I move about the stage. I point to them; smile at them; talk to them; sing to them. It's about connecting, making each fan feel like I am performing for her and her alone.

Part of it is making sure that the venue transforms into a party. When I come onto the stage, the fans stand up and cheer, clap, wave. They are just as excited to see me as I am to be in their presence. We have a bond. I implore the crowd: "Somebody scream!!!" And guess what? They scream.

I start out in a suit and, before long, I am so deeply involved in the performance that my body heat rises. Of course, that means I have to take off my jacket. But I don't just take it off. I slowly, tantalizingly release it from my body, playing to my female-dominated audience. They cheer.

I ask the crowd to sing along with me, and they do. Most times, I do not even ask them to sing along. They do it because we have created a connection—they are with me up there on stage.

A lot of time, thought, and energy goes into that stage production; a lot of heart and soul, too. So, why am I telling you this? Because all that we put into our performances at work—whether it is on stage, a presentation in front of peers, a sales pitch to clients, etc.—we must put that and even *more* into our relationships.

In a sense, maintaining a relationship is very much a performance. You should be about impressing your mate, no matter how long you have been together and despite your thoughts that "he ain't going nowhere."

It's about turning that mentality around. Look at the most important times on your job, *any* job. If you are a carpenter and the owner of the company decides to ride with you to your jobs that day, you are going to hammer that cabinet with more vigor than ever and communicate with the customer clearly and pleasantly—if you want to keep your job.

If you have an interview for a promotion, you will come looking your best, totally knowledgeable about the position, prepared for every question—if you want to get the job.

It is the same thing with a relationship. I have grown to where my performance with the woman in my life gets just as much time and commitment to perfection that my performance on stage or in the studio receives.

If that sounds like I'm calling a relationship a job, it's because I *am*. You've heard it before over and over, I'm sure: Relationships are hard work. That's a truism that will always hold up. However, it doesn't have to be unpleasant work. Ever had a job you were excited to go to every day, a job that did not *seem* like a job? If you haven't, well, I feel bad for you. But if you have, then that's how a good, healthy relationship should feel: like a job that you are eager to get to; a job you put your heart and soul into; a job that fulfills you; a job that requires your best and consistent effort. When it is that kind of job, it does not seem like work. It seems, and feels, like the right thing to do.

When I perform, I have a backlog of dozens and dozens of songs to choose from for the show. If I did all of them, I would be on for four hours—with no opening acts. So, I have to go through a thorough process of selecting songs that will convey and capture the mood I want to create.

I want to make you croon and make you dance and make you, well, sweat. I have an objective when I choreograph the show. Not choreograph from a dance routine standpoint, but choreograph from a tactical standpoint of what songs will be performed, in what order and how.

It should be the same way you deal with your relationship. If he is worthy, you should have a list of objectives to letting him know how much you care, how much he means to you, how attracted you are to him—whatever it is that you would like to convey. You should choreograph how you want an evening to go, how you want to exist with your partner. Have a well-thought-out plan. Now, don't get it twisted: I'm not talking about a scheme to trick someone, or to be disingenuous. I'm talking about a course of action to take to make sure you are nourishing your relationship.

If it were involving work, you would stay up at night making sure your stuff was together. That's the same attitude that has to prevail with your man. If you do, just as you get that promotion on the J.O.B., your relationship will reap all kinds of rewards.

KEITH'S KEY: It would be helpful to lose the mentality that the phrase "relationships are hard work" is a negative one. Almost every time I hear someone say that, it is expressed with such exasperation and frustration. When you look at it as a burden, you are less likely to put your all into it because you resent the entire notion. You get tired before you even put in the work. So much of what we do and how we receive things is psychological. I'm no psychologist, but you don't have to be one to know the power of the mind. I have experienced enough to know that your mind can take you places you don't need to go.

So, since you can control your thoughts, try looking at putting in work on your relationship at home as something positive and wonderful. View it as more valuable than your job—and it is, by the way. Look at your relationship as something that needs your attention, effort and work to thrive. Act like you are on stage, performing for your partner, putting him in a place of comfort and love. That mentality will carry you a long way—and make your mate happy.

And we know what should happen with a happy mate; he should reciprocate. He should be inspired to put in the work, effort and time into you. Two people working together for a common goal produces remarkable results. It's the same premise as two people moving a boulder. One person doing all the work makes for a tough, nearly impossible feat.

But two of you pushing in the same direction, together, as one, get the boulder where you want it to be much easier and much quicker. They say "two heads are better than one," and that's true. But two people working on the relationship with the same energy and passion as you do your job increases the chances of great results.

CHAPTER SEVEN

KEEP YOUR BUSINESS AS *YOUR* BUSINESS

L adies, one of the Cardinal sins so many of you commit with your girl-friends is letting them too far into your relationship life. They can recite, chapter and verse, all the intricacies of your man's habits, skills, weak-nesses, strengths and anything else that relates to what you have with him.

You share with them all your troubles, pleasures, issues and concerns. And many of you even share how skilled your man is as a lover—a serious mistake.

And you know why that's wrong? Because that's none of their business. Period. More than that, those "friends" many times use that information against you. How? Why?

Well, start with the fact that it is definitely true that misery loves company. You know how many times I've heard from females that their "friend" advised them in some crazy way about their men?

Case in point: A female friend got into an argument with her mate over him not returning her call after an hour. He said he was busy on a confer-ence call. She called her girlfriend and gave her the blow-by-blow. Instead of getting back rational, mature advice, her girlfriend gave her extreme nonsense: "I wouldn't take that, girl. You need to fire him. You can't trust him; he probably was with some bitch. And if he calls you to apologize, you shouldn't even accept it. Make him beg."

And what made it worse was the woman—a seemingly intelligent young lady—actually did what her "friend" advised, even though her "friend" had not been in a successful relationship since who-knew-when. She hadn't even been on a real date in a year. And any relationship she did have was marred in drama. But she had all the answers. And yet, she was still the go-to person for this woman, someone she relied on to guide her through the landmines of her relationship. Now, how backward is that?

That "friend" with the whack advice is the very last person you need to go to for relationship advice. She's miserable in her own life and as much as she declares, "You're my girl," there is a silent hate in her that you have a man and a relationship and she does not. It's better for her psyche that you both be bitter and single rather than just her.

If I have heard it once I've heard it a hundred times—a woman suddenly shocked when a friend and confidante shows herself to be a hater. She hates you and the fact that you have a relationship and she doesn't. And you are the one who fuels the hate by sharing your intimate relationship details. You give her the ammunition to cause havoc in your life, as she is not interested in helping you fix any troubling situation.

Of course, this does not apply to all women. Some friends are die-hard, true friends who appreciate you sharing your private information, and they offer sound advice or none at all; they become sounding boards and support systems. But they are not the norm.

The worst-case scenario has happened so many times, probably even to you. How do you think there are countless cases of where your man ends up with your "friend"? Sometimes it's because the man is sorry and a loser and pursues her. And she's immoral enough to accept his advances.

But most cases occur because of *you*. *You* are the one who told your "friend" about how your man pleased you in bed, about your sexual exploits, and his bedroom skill set. It is you who let her into your bedroom. And she, being the hater that she is, takes that information and uses it against you.

All you did is pique her curiosity, make her feel like she should have what you have. So, she makes her move on your man. She even tells him that she knows how good he is in bed because *you* told her.

Next thing you know, she's bragging to you about how she's slept with your man. And then she does the ultimate—she lets you know it was your sharing of your business that made her interested in *your* man. And it is then that you finally realize you should have kept your mouth shut.

If this sounds dramatic to you, then you probably have not run across the numerous scandalous "friends" who will do anything they can to get their hands on a man, any man.

I have had so many occasions when women knew I was married, or in a relationship, and it did not matter—they wanted what they wanted. That's the attitude of a lot of females. And when you tell them all your business, that opens them up to really feeling like there is a weakness in your relationship that they can pounce on.

Just as crazy to me is this scenario: I told a woman once that her girlfriend came on to me, straight up offered herself to me. I could have taken it and run and the woman I was involved with would have never known. But I did the right thing: I told my lady that her "friend" had propositioned me and really was not her friend.

Instead of thanking me for my honesty, she refused to believe me. No way would her girl betray her like that. Instead, she got angry with me and told me it was my ego that made me misinterpret her friend's actions.

"You probably came on to her," she had the audacity to say.

When I asked her to confront her friend, she told me that she wouldn't. "I won't even embarrass myself by telling her that," she said.

Wow, I thought. It was clear by what her "friend" had said to me that my lady was telling her everything about us. And yet, she could not put her arms around the fact that she could be betrayed by someone she trusted—but she *could* believe that I was lying.

She said, "You just don't like her. You don't want us to be friends."

She was right about that. I saw in the woman that there was something unscrupulous about her and I was right. But my lady could not see it. Needless to say, the relationship died rather quickly.

What is it in a woman that compels her to share intimate relationship details with her friends? Is it the need to tell her business? Insecurity? Silliness and immaturity? Well, it's probably a little bit of all that.

But you know what? Guys do it, too. Probably not as much as women, but men run their mouths about their women to their boys and it does nothing to help the relationships.

I have had a case where I actually told a guy I thought was my man about a woman and the next thing I know, he was hollering at her. Thankfully, she told me about it and I confronted "my man" and let him know that wasn't proper. Of course, he tried to deny it. But that was my lesson—that was the last time I gave up personal information to anyone about a woman I was involved with.

In some cases, you don't have to even tell your business. I had a guy who hung out with me and it turned out he felt some kind of way about me because he shared things about what I did or said while out with the woman, giving her the impression that I was doing wrong by her. That's a lesson on being mindful of the company you keep.

Some of my other friends sensed something about this one person, but I thought they were being paranoid. I said, "Nah, he's all right." In reality, I was too close to see what they saw, which was that he had a level of "hate" with him that was apparent to them. Finally, it showed itself when he went back to a woman and thought he was telling my business to her. It was shocking at first because I just didn't see that in this guy. He was cool, or so I thought. But he actually had something against me to the point where he thought he could use what he knew about me against me with a woman. How weak was that?

Thankfully, the woman was mature and focused more on the fact that he was a hater than the crap he had told her. She called me to tell me that my "friend" was not my friend.

Then there was the case of one of my supposed "boys" that I trusted hollering at a lady I was dating. Worse, any intimate detail I told him about her, he shared with her. It actually was very hurtful to the woman because it was information that only I could have known, meaning she realized that I gave him too many details about our situation, and about her.

She was very upset with me, to the point where it hindered our relationship. The guy's intent was to break us up so he could step in. Didn't happen. I learned my hard lesson, that your business is your business. When you open up to some people—not all, but some—you could be putting yourself in a compromising position.

From that point on, I have been mindful of the people I allow in my circle. Everyone you meet is not your friend. And, for sure, everyone you know is not worthy of you sharing your business. Hardly anyone is, actually.

On another note relating to telling your business, I am not interested in hearing about past relationships of the woman I'm dealing with—unless she has something that would impact my health. Other than that, keep it to yourself.

Ladies seem to think the new men in their lives want to hear about the old men. Not. Don't ever tell me, "My old man did this or did that." How is that helping me?

What that man did to you, how he treated or mistreated you, or how you all got along or did not get along, matters not one bit to me. And if you're telling me about how good he was to you, then I have one question: Why aren't you still with him?

I'm not asking about those you dated in the past and you don't need to volunteer that info to me. Really, it's not the kind of information that makes a man feel better about who you are.

Of course, there are some guys who will ask for all the details they can get about your past, as if you're going to give them the full truth or as if that information will give them an honest insight about what they are getting into. I don't see the point.

Unless you're telling me about contracting a sexually transmitted disease—especially HIV—I don't need to know how many old boyfriends you had, what you all did, anything.

I recall a woman trying to make me jealous or feel an urgency about getting with her when she started naming celebrities she either dated or who were interested in dating her. She was fine and I had an interest in her. But she didn't need to drop names like that.

It made her seem cheap and like I was shallow enough to really want her because she had dated popular people. In reality, it turned me off. It made me feel like she was a groupie, a gold digger, or someone who was not pure. I don't mean pure like a virgin, but that she was not someone of pure thoughts about herself. She was insecure and needed to associate with people she considered to have a celebrity status in order to make her feel a particular way about herself. So, needless to say, there was no building of a relationship with her.

The flip side of not wanting to hear about someone's past is that I don't see the value in me telling a woman about ladies of my past. I'm not going there. That information would not help you really get to know me. So, I don't volunteer it and I have told women straight up, "It's none of your business," if they asked specific questions about my past relationships.

When getting a relationship going in the right direction, the attitude has to be about getting to know that person through your own means—not through what may or may not have happened in previous relationships, and definitely not through examining the partners of the past.

KEITH'S KEY: Understand that telling the intimate details of your relationship to your friends is a sure-fire way to create drama. It's none of their business. And people are so hateful that they often will intentionally give you advice that will hurt your relationship.

If you're especially unlucky, that "friend"—armed with inside information about your mate provided by you—will even pursue your man. In some cases, a true, smart, committed friend offers sound, mature advice that could help you through a challenging scenario with your partner. But even that friend should not be privileged to intimate details of your relationship.

Bottom line, if you simply cannot help yourself and must speak about your man, you have to understand who you are speaking with. Choose your friends—and lean on them—wisely.

CHAPTER EIGHT

COMMUNICATION:
DON'T TALK AT ME, TALK TO ME

You've heard before that communication is an important part of every relationship. Not only is that true, but especially today, where people seem to be more sensitive than ever, it is critical that you communicate in a way that is direct and respectful.

In other words, it's not just *what* you say, but *how* you say it. That's really the key to effective communication, right? Think about it: If your man says, "Get me a beer," I'm sure you would receive it better if he had said, "Could you get me a beer, please?"

It sounds better, nicer, and it makes the other person more willing to extend themselves.

If he's going to pick you up to go to a movie, it's better if you say, "I will be ready on time, honey," instead of saying, "Don't be late."

You feel me on that? You see the difference in the two? One is pleasant and reassuring; the other is a command that most people will take offense to, causing stress.

It's all about the words we choose and how we deliver them that makes communication something that provides comfort and not drama. No matter how comfortable you are with someone or how long you have been with him, you just cannot get so lax that your communication methods deteriorate. If you started off speaking pleasantly to your mate, it stands to reason that he would expect you to continue speaking to him that way. When you think about it, that's only fair.

So, why do so many people get complacent over time and feel like it is unnecessary to make the effort to speak to your significant other in a caring way? The improper tone or inflection in your voice can lead to arguments or bad attitudes. I'm pointing this out because sometimes we don't even realize how we come at each other.

I recall a woman once telling me to "stop by on your way to my house and pick up some champagne." Now, the idea of me bringing some champagne to her house was a good one; I liked it, but the way her suggestion came across was like a demand. That didn't work for me.

So, of course, I let her know that, and an argument followed. I did not pick up the champagne and it was all because of how she had spoken to me. I didn't appreciate it and it led to drama.

Now, let's keep it real: Some people like drama. Some people thrive off of it. Some people even feel like if there is no drama, then you don't really care about them. That's some crazy stuff, but it's true. I've heard it before. I've experienced it before. And you have, too. In fact, you might be one of those people who believe drama equates to love.

Well, I'm here to tell you that it does not. It equates to crazy. I'm just saying…Let the drama go. It does nothing to enhance your life. Try to create harmony through the way you communicate with each other. When a woman starts talking *at* me and not *to* me, I check out immediately. I'm gone. Done. Why? There is clearly a lack of respect being shown to me, which I would not tolerate from anyone. And you should not accept it, either.

Simply put, we have to communicate with each other on a level of respect first and foremost. If you want to be heard, the best way to accomplish that is to be mindful of how you confront someone. And that's just not me. Most everyone blocks out what you have to say when you are attacking and accusatory and disrespectful.

Even in your most heated or uncomfortable moments, you have to address your man in a way that does not put him on the defensive. The louder you get, or the more attacking you get, the more loud and attacking he will get. And then what do you accomplish? Nothing.

How many times have you been in a heated argument and then upset with someone for days, and when you have to sit back and remember what started it, you can't think of a thing? Many times, right? I have been there. And usually it was because of how someone spoke to you, which led to an argument that grew and grew for no real reason.

WORDS CAN DEFINITELY HURT YOU

There is beauty in today's technology and then there is the beast of it, too. When you're being romantic and sexy with text messaging or e-mailing, it is easy to see how those instant methods of communication can heighten a relationship. Shoot, there are people who have met on an Internet dating site and have fallen in love though e-mails and text messages alone. I need human contact, face-to-face connection, to feel like I am getting to know someone. But to each his own; everyone is different.

My point is, as great as it can be to send e-mails or text messages, it should not be your primary mode of communication in attempting to start, rekindle, or maintain a relationship. Not that there is much wrong with doing so. It, in fact, can be a big help.

But many times you cannot determine the tone or attitude of the sender, leaving you to interpret the message. And when that happens, well, it can turn ugly.

Say you're texting back and forth about getting together. Suddenly, you text, *"I want to have fun tonight."* You smile as you text it, as it is a playful message.

You man receives it but cannot determine the playfulness. Instead, he takes it to mean you think he is not fun—or has not been fun while you were out. So, he gets on the defensive.

"If I'm not fun, you can go by yourself."

Now you're offended. You think: "Why would he let me go out by myself?" So, you text him back. *"Maybe I should go by myself."*

And he fires back. *"Whatever."*

And now you're fuming. And your plans for a fun night out are blown because he misinterpreted your text message. The lesson: Sometimes it pays to punch the keys and get a voice on the phone because when you hear the inflection in someone's voice, you know when he is joking or serious, angry or upset.

Above all, when it comes to communication, it's about, well, communicating. I'm no psychologist, but I've lived long enough, experienced enough, and talked to enough people to know that communication breakdowns kill relationships. Period.

We have to get past being upset and holding in whatever it is that's bothering us. In my case, if I'm bothered and don't let it out, it builds up and builds up. Suddenly, it's not something minor anymore. Now, after letting it fester in me for so long, it becomes something major, something that creates a bad feeling inside me, which is never good.

The longer you hold in a concern, the bigger it becomes. You know what I'm saying? No?

Okay, here's an example. This woman bothered me by her consistent disregard for what I had to do. No matter what, she wanted me to pick her up. Now, I'm as much a gentleman as the next guy and I don't mind picking up a date. But there were times when I needed her to meet me so we could get to a particular place at a reasonable time.

Well, she told me one day that she didn't feel like driving and, basically, whatever I was doing should be pushed aside to come across town to pick her up. Well, that bothered me a lot. I felt like she totally disregarded the fact that I had things to do that day, which did not make me feel good about her.

But I did not express my concerns. I tried to keep the peace and move on with her. Well, the next incident came—she sat and talked to her girlfriend for an extended period on the cell phone while we were out at dinner—and, again, I was bothered but did not say anything.

A week or so later, another incident occurred—she told me to come over for dinner and, when I got there, she "decided" it would be best that we go out to dinner. And, of course, when the bill came, she totally ignored it.

Now, taken individually, each of those three incidents should not have been a big deal. If I had addressed each one at the time, we likely could have had a conversation about it, cleared things up, and moved on without any built-up animosity.

But because I held them in, they became lumped together and became one really big situation that made me angry. Really angry. Lumped together, I saw the situations as a lack of respect on her part, which I could not tolerate. So, a big argument followed by me laying down my issues one-by-one.

She was genuinely surprised that I brought up incidents from many weeks before. But that's how it goes when you don't communicate what's on your mind and heart at that time. You hold it in and those minor incidents become major. Then you have three "major" incidents stacking on top of each other, giving you the feeling of one really big problem.

Needless to say, when another minor incident happened, it felt like a major thing because those other three issues were never addressed, and an argument was the result. Also, that was the end of our dating—all over me not coming forward when I was first bothered about something that could have been smoothed over at that time.

When my anger subsided, I realized that it all could have been prevented—IF I had communicated my concerns when they happened. See, the key to communication is not just to talk; it's also about talking about what should be talked about when you have something on your mind and heart.

KEITH'S KEY: Think constantly about expressing yourself in a way that would make the receiver embrace what you have to convey. It would be counterproductive to communicate openly, but be abrasive or insensitive to your mate's feelings. That's the quickest way to get someone to shut down on you.

Do not hold back when you are bothered by something, someone, a situation. Address it head on and immediately—but do it with tact and diplomacy. Do not come off as arrogant; humility is a redeeming quality. Do not accuse your mate of what you do not know; instead, pose your concerns in a question to elicit a response.

Be mindful that not communicating is equivalent to shutting down a relationship, for all the pent-up concerns, issues or dislikes that you have will come rushing out like a waterfall, and you can almost always count on that turning the mate into a fisherman, trying to get to shore after his boat turned over. Do yourself and your relationship a favor by taking the time out to talk to each other with love and respect, even when you totally disagree on a particular subject.

CHAPTER NINE

BEING HUMBLE MAKES A DIFFERENCE

A s cute as you are and as funny and smart and sexy and nice as you are…guess what? You are NOT perfect. Sorry to burst your bubble, but POP. You're *not* perfect.

And you know what else? No one is, which means we all make mistakes. So, as perfect as you believe you are, you do things—intentionally or not—to the mate in your life that he does not like, or even deserve.

That's a normal transgression. The real point is: When those occasions occur, what do you do?

Do you immediately regret being something less than your man needed you to be at that time? Or do you wild out, get defensive, and create an argument? Or do you do the simplest and right thing: apologize?

That seems like a logical thing, right? But most people have a problem apologizing. And you know why? Because they think they are perfect. They just cannot face up to someone actually considering that they are less than perfect. They will do anything, create any distraction, come up with any excuse…anything to prevent from apologizing.

If "I love you" are the words everyone wants to hear, "I'm sorry" are the words most people are uncomfortable saying.

Of course, not everyone is this way. Some of us find it easy to apologize. Some of us might find it difficult to do but do it anyway because we realize it is the right thing to do. And then there are some of us who apologize but do so with so much hesitation that it does not come off as sincere.

That's almost as bad as no apology at all. You know what I'm saying? I can tell you from experience where a woman was dead wrong but she didn't see it, even after I pointed out all the details to her. Finally, she offered a smack in my face—a half-hearted apology.

Without getting too specific about the incident (you know, protect the guilty), it was a case where she insulted me by questioning how much time I spent with her versus me handling my fatherly responsibilities with my kids. Now, that was reason for me to go off on her, but I have learned to compose myself and handle situations better as I get older.

Instead, as patiently as possible, I explained to her that no one comes before my kids—and that she should always respect that, and that it was disrespectful that she would come at me about spending time with my children. She seemed to listen to me, but I waited for the words to make me feel better about her. I told her, "So, understanding my position on this, is there something you'd like to say to me?"

She looked at me for a few seconds. Then she said, "Not really. I understand what you're saying."

I was like, "Really? If you do understand, don't you think you should say a little more than that?"

"More? No, I don't."

I only wanted to hear two words from her to allow me to feel like she was not a self-centered, egomaniacal narcissist. But she refused to say them.

"Don't you think you should apologize to me?" I finally asked her. I tried giving her every reason to see it for herself, but she didn't.

"I don't understand," she said. "I mean, I understand your position. But I was giving you my opinion. Why should I apologize? I wasn't wrong about anything. I had an opinion, which I am entitled to."

Of course, that did not sit well with me, and I let her know it.

"Yes, but your opinion insulted me," I said. "I explained to you that it's disrespectful to me when you tell me that I need to put my kids down to find time for you. You don't see that as something wrong?"

"It's not wrong," she said. "It was my opinion."

Instead of going off, I continued to try to make things clear to her. I said, "But I just told you I was offended and disrespected by your opinion. To me, that's cause for you to apologize."

"Well, if I offended you, I apologize," she said with much attitude.

Did you catch that? That was a back-handed, half-hearted apology if I ever heard one.

"What do you mean, *if* you offended me? I told you that you did," I said.

"And I apologized," she fired back.

This went on for another few minutes before I finally ended it by saying, "Okay, you don't want to apologize. That's the bottom line. You think whatever you say is right and so, even when someone tells you repeatedly that you were offensive, you still refuse to see it.

"If the positions were reversed, I would apologize simply because you told me that I offended you. Period. I would do that because I don't want to offend you. That's what friends do—they apologize when they should. You should apologize to me."

She looked at me as if I asked her to change the oil in my car. So, we had a staring match for a few seconds. Finally, she said, "I'm sorry. I wasn't trying to offend you."

It took a bunch of effort to get that out of her mouth. By then, I knew all I needed to know about her, and it wasn't good.

Know this: There is power in a sincere apology. It frees you of the burden of having—intentionally or not—wronged someone. It shows humility, but is a very redeeming quality. And it shows that you care enough about the person to humble yourself.

I have been around so-called celebrities who have a real problem being humble, who believe their way is the only way and that their word is the law. It's a ridiculous position to take for anyone. They will show up late for appointments, be rude to people around them and never bother to apologize. It makes me shake my head.

It is a much more likable trait to be humble, to show humility. In relationships, being humble often can calm a troublesome situation that you have created. Think about it: We all have had situations blown out of proportion when they could have been controlled if we had just apologized. Two words: "I'm sorry."

When you make your mate mad and have no real defense for it, the only words that give you a chance of making things better is a sincere apology. Note the word "sincere." A sincere apology should disarm anyone because, ultimately, what do you have left but an apology? The deed has been done. You cannot reverse it. So you have to mend it, and the best way to begin doing that is to give a heartfelt apology, i.e., "I'm really sorry, baby. It won't happen again."

To begrudgingly apologize is the same as making things worse. It's like you're doing it because you are almost forced to, not because it's the right thing to do. That only makes your better half more upset.

It comes down to that word again: "humility." When you are humble, you readily apologize for any wrongdoing. You do it because it is the right thing to admit your fault and want to make things better.

KEITH'S KEY: The best way I can put it is to put yourself in your mate's place when he is upset with you about something, big or small. Take your own feelings out of the equation. Try your hardest to look at things from his position. If his stance has merit and you honestly put yourself in his place, you will more readily offer an apology for a given situation. No way around it: It's the right thing to do. Sometimes people make us so angry that we say things we should not say—things that, in that split second, we mean. But once we settle down, we wish we had those evil words back. You cannot get them back. But you can offer a deep, heartfelt, sincere apology to try to lessen their impact.

Of course, the best way to avoid having to apologize is to never do anything wrong. But then, you'd have to be perfect to achieve that, and we know no one's perfect. Right?

CHAPTER TEN
FIDELITY MUST BE A PRIORITY

When you go through something with someone you love, the emotions run crazy. And depending on how bad it gets, you could think the best thing to do is to seek comfort from someone else. Bad move.

Being unfaithful is the No. 1 cause of trouble and breakups of relationships. If you really examine all the angles before acting, you would make another choice. To do so requires you to take emotion out of the situation, which isn't easy when you are upset or disappointed.

But acting on emotion by turning to someone else only complicates matters. Putting a third (or, in some cases, fourth or fifth) person into your turmoil only messes up even more what you are contending with.

Someone might say it would be payback for being wronged, as if you actually would feel better after having given your body up to someone who is not your mate because you were mad. That's borderline whorish, right?

When a situation comes down the pike that hurts you, it requires you to stand up for yourself, not lie down. It has taken me a while to come to this, but I understand it now: We are products of the people we sleep with.

That's not a good thing to consider, is it? Makes you feel a little creepy? But it is true. The good thing is that we can overcome our dumb decisions by not making more dumb decisions, especially as payback for being angry.

In reality, that is the worst thing you could do on so many levels. One, it's just dead wrong. You cheapen who you are and your self-worth by taking such an immature step. You turned yourself into a "jump off," and, as such, you could be sure that you would never elevate to anything beyond that.

No man worth his shoes would take a woman who was a "jump off" and make her his exclusive woman. And you know why? It's simple: He would have no respect for you. He would have no faith that you would not do to him what you did to the other guy. It would hang over you like a dark cloud. You'd be lost, And confused.

There has been more than one woman in my life who thought giving up their body to me meant I would be all about them. But they were so wrong. Especially with people who are so-called celebrities; we constantly have in the back of our minds whether someone new we meet is interested in us, or us as well-known people. There's a big difference.

When you're interested in someone and have sex with that person for reasons other than love or some very serious "like," you set yourself up for failure and major disappointment. You will not receive what you think you deserve because he looks at you in a way that is not respectful or flattering. In the end—and the end could come quickly or he could drag it out thirteen years as Herman Cain did—you will feel empty and hurt and will regret making that choice.

Still, the biggest reason, though, to hold on to fidelity is because it is the right thing to do. So many times we fail at a simple thing: Do what you *know* is right. It can't get much simpler than that, right? You know what to do…I do it!!!

But most of us—myself included—too often go another route. We find doing the right thing either boring or not a strong enough statement. So we take those unfaithful steps that end up hurting us in one way or another down the line, And it could have easily been avoided.

Being faithful shows respect for your partner, the person you have committed yourself to either by marriage or by your word. Or both. To dishonor that person with infidelity is a pretty low move.

It is an awful feeling to do something so hurtful to someone and have to deal with the pain you caused him. It's a selfish act that could have been avoided with patience, perspective, and sound judgment.

To get there requires a level of maturity and discipline that most of us just do not have—or are afraid to exercise. It takes all that to make controlled decisions and not fly-off-the-handle, emotional moves that blow up everything.

Like everything else in this book, I realize firsthand how poor choices around infidelity do nothing to benefit a relationship. As someone in the spotlight, I have gotten all kinds of propositions from women, women who knew I was married or in a relationship. They just didn't care.

I'm not proud to reveal this, but I definitely took advantage of my share of those women. And some of those times I was in a relationship, making it doubly wrong.

Sometimes, because I sensed the woman I was dealing with had not been honest with me, I convinced myself that it was appropriate to get with someone else to make us even. How dumb and immature was that?

On top of that, it did not make me feel good. It did not take away the feelings I had about the first woman. So, it was all so meaningless. "Getting back" at someone by hooking up with someone else makes as much sense as being unfaithful in the first place. It's dumb.

And even in the cases where the women were wrong, pursuing me knowing I was committed somewhere else, the bigger responsibility was on me to do right thing, the mature thing, as the one who was in a relationship at the time. I should have made a stronger, more level-headed, wiser choice. But instead of acting from a rational position, I acted on emotion. That will get us in trouble every time.

You ever hear someone say to step back and take a deep breath and count to ten before responding to something that could be emotional? It's said for a reason. The farther away we get from a troubling situation, the clearer and more rational we become, which allows us to make smarter decisions that are not designed to hurt someone.

Emotion is great. It's awesome—when used in the proper way. To be so emotional about something to where you abandon your morals, to where you dismiss what you know is right, well, that's a bit too emotional, don't you think?

So that leads us back to the best methodology being the faithful approach. It's direct and honest. Honoring a relationship with fidelity leaves open the opportunity to rescue it from trouble because there would not be an outside emotion to deal with, no third person that would surely get in the way of your thoughts and feelings. Clarity and perspective allow you the opportunity to look at your situation without clouds or obstructions.

What are clouds and obstructions? They are people you have put into your mix, people who likely now have an emotional investment into you and therefore have an emotional response that further widens the gap in your relationship.

Example: I hooked up with this girl—really cute, seemingly cool—because this woman I was dating was shady. I couldn't prove it and didn't try to prove it, but I felt it. So, I thought I'd break my commitment by doing what I believed she was doing.

Well, in the end, I felt no better about her and worse about myself. And, the other woman believed she was entitled to give me drama because I slept with her. So, instead of doing something to mend the problems I had with the woman I was dating, I made it even unhealthier by breaking my fidelity and getting another woman's emotions involved.

On top of that, I was operating from a position of guilt. It did not feel good to know I had betrayed the woman I was involved with and I felt bad that I had drawn another woman into my unsettled situation. It was a bad spot. But the turmoil I felt could have been totally avoided if I had taken the smart, mature and RIGHT approach of discussion instead of an emotional reaction.

What I have since learned to do is take a simple approach: positive over negative.

That's not to suggest being blind to obvious problems or concerns that may arise. But the most effective way to deal with them is by focusing on the positive—or doing the positive thing.

In the case of fidelity, the positive thing is to hold on to it. It keeps you honest, on the up-and-up. It shows strength and maturity. And it shows you care. Going outside the relationship does the opposite; showing deceit, weakness, immaturity and selfishness.

It is a positive approach to be strong and mature. I have listened to thousands and thousands of callers who hit me up on my radio show, "The Sweat Hotel," and the majority of them come with a negative attitude. That negativity clouds any thoughts for a reasonable resolution. It's all about revenge and anger and paying someone back and anything that does not help you look at the situation in a rational way.

Am I the only one who encounters people with so much negative energy that they turn your attitude? Surely, I cannot be the only one. Many people perpetuate bad vibes every day through their attitudes. That attitude carries over to how you deal with not only the person who made you angry, but also to everyone else you come in contact with. And that makes you a person no one really wants to be around because you're draining the energy out of anyone you encounter.

See, lots of times, people don't even see or realize the negativity they carry with them and spread to everyone else. That attitude does nothing to promote peace and harmony. In fact, it does the opposite: It brings down those you consider friends.

You cannot be blamed for someone else's infidelity. That would be a decision he made and him only. But you can inspire thoughts kinds of thoughts into someone's mind by carrying negative energy into every conversation or situation. I mean, I know some women who bring all kinds of drama with them no matter the subject, situation, or scenario.

You see all the good in that person, but their negativity is so strong that it makes you want to get away from him. And sometimes getting away from him means getting with someone else. It's not right and it's not their fault that you made such a selfish, immature decision. But a more positive outlook could breed a more comfortable environment, making your mate less frustrated and less interested in looking someplace else for comfort.

Look, I know: Some guys are going to do what they want to do, even if you are the most kind and pleasant and passionate person around. But not all. You ask a man why he's out there and many will tell you he's seeking an escape from the negativity that his woman brings. Right or wrong, unfair or not, that's real talk for some men.

KEITH'S KEY: Take the commitment of fidelity as seriously as you would the most important thing in your life, because it is that important. No matter how troubled your relationship may be, bringing someone else into the situation will only complicate it, not help it. It is a selfish, immature, and irresponsible action that you ultimately will regret.

Infidelity not only impacts you. It damages your mate and clouds your judgment—and all but destroys trust in your relationship. On top of that, it dishonors your man, making him feel less than his worth and likely pushing him to do the same in retaliation.

Lastly, a third party is now mixed up in your relationship, which can never be productive. That extra person's emotions can get involved, making for a potentially messy situation.

So, take the positive approach over negative. Talk to your mate, reason with him, fall back on your morals—anything other than cheapening yourself by being unfaithful. Trust me, it will not help the situation. In fact, it will eventually destroy it.

CHAPTER ELEVEN

WHO IS THE RIGHT PERSON FOR YOU???

Perhaps the ultimate process of determining how to make your relationship last forever is to understand that you are with the right person for you. Not the right person to your mom, or your friends, or even your children. You should not settle for someone because they are in your immediate space, interested, and available. That's the fail-safe way of having a miserable existence, faking it with someone you recognize in your heart is not even remotely suitable for you.

So, how do you do that? How do you know who is right for you? For men, it cannot be about, as New Edition sang, "a big butt and a smile." It can't be about a little butt and a frown, either. But no way can I deny that the physical matters. It matters a lot.

They say men are visual creatures, which is true. I know me: I'm looking at all aspects of a woman's physical appearance. Her hair has to be on point—it shows she cares about how she shows up, which is important to me. She has to be into fashion—not necessarily spending crazy money on designer clothes. That's not necessary.

But it is necessary to have a sense of what looks good on her and what would attract a man's eye. That does not mean tight clothes exposing every curve of her body, short skirts that reveal too much skin, or blouses that make her cleavage look like overblown balloons.

Tasteful is always the best route. There are men who respond to all that extra stuff. But you attract a particular kind of man with the way you dress. It kills me every time I encounter a woman who complains about a man staring at her when she's wearing clothes so tight she could get a blood clot. When you dress that way, that's what you get.

The older you get the more you understand what you are really attracted to. And to fall for someone strictly because of physical attributes does not establish a long-lasting, productive relationship.

The same goes for women. Women are less concerned with the physical than men, but not by much. Every time a woman sees a photo of a guy who obviously works out with his shirt off, you hear all the same reactions you hear from men when they see a big-butt woman.

Again ladies, hitching your wagon to a guy only because he's eye candy could be setting yourself up for disappointment. No matter how hard you try to ignore elements of the person that do not work for you, you will not be able to—not for long.

Don't get me wrong now; there is nothing wrong with eye candy. But that eye candy needs to be supplemented with qualities that really matter to you. I mean, what is a good-looking person with no core? A mannequin, that's what.

So, let's be sure that eye candy is not hollow, that the muscle-bound man you are so physically attracted to is sensitive to your needs, has ambition, has a brain and knows how to use it. Make sure that he cares about your kids and that he's not selfish and in love with himself so much that he does not show how much he loves you.

Know what I'm saying? Listen, I have met—and dated—some women that most men (and even some women) would consider "fine." But once I got to know some of them, I learned that the mental package needed to hold my interest was practically nonexistent. They realized they were beautiful and they relied totally on that beauty. They did not think it was necessary to comprehend what was going on in the world or to be a warm person or an unselfish person or just a nice person. Enough men had spoiled them and allowed them to simply be an attractive arm piece to the point that they had no idea how to be more.

There was this one woman who was a head-turner. If you wanted to talk to her about the latest designer or the best places to shop in Los Angeles, or New York, she could go on and on. She could even break down the differences between a Sable mink coat and a Chinchilla.

She also had a list of the top restaurants in all the major cities in her

BlackBerry. And she could easily recite the airport codes for all the cities since men flew her around the country so they could impress others by showing up with her on their arms.

But if you asked her about anything significant in the world, she had nothing to offer. She couldn't speak intelligently about the Presidential race. She was clueless on anything regarding the wars in the Middle East. She had no coherent opinion on the death penalty. In short, she was a beautiful idiot.

This is not to say it is required to be a genius or someone who is an expert on political or world affairs. But it only make sense that, as a person living in the world, you understand a little about what's going on in it. It makes sense that you watch the news at least on occasion, pick up a newspaper, or go to a newspaper's website to have some sense of what's happening outside of your own world.

When I suggested to this woman that she consider expanding her knowledge, she told me that she had a college degree and that the news was depressing. I concede that it can be depressing to watch the first ten minutes of the news, with all the crime that has dominated our society. But that, to me anyway, should never prohibit you from being out of the loop on matters that concern you and how the world functions.

So, while the woman was gorgeous with a perfectly sculpted body to match, she would have been a disaster for me to be in a relationship with. She would have fulfilled the physical side that matters. But all the other things that bothered me about her—selfishness, shallowness, and disinterest in anything outside of her world—would have killed the relationship before too long.

Someone else—maybe someone equally shallow—would have found her as an ideal mate for the rest of their lives. But for me, I needed more. And that's all right. It's acceptable to be picky. In fact, you MUST be picky.

As a so-called celebrity, I have the problem of trying to discern if a woman is interested in me because of Keith Sweat the entertainer, or Keith Sweat the man. In most cases, I might meet a woman because they are familiar with my music. But I'm sure they go through a process of figuring out if I have substance to my character. (Well, some of them do; some don't care. We call them groupies.)

What I'm saying is this: The majority of the time, our relationship troubles stem from making bad selections on the people we allow into our lives. And we're all guilty of it.

Raise your hand if you got involved with, or even married, someone you did not exactly feel totally in touch with. My hand is up!!!

What happens is that we tend to see what we like and give it more weight than some things that bother us. We believe we can get beyond those things. After all, they're not that big of a deal. He might smoke, even though you might think it's a disgusting habit.

She might have kids and you do not like the way she allows them to run over her. He might have a decent job but trouble managing money. He might like to go out and party and you might prefer intimate, at-home time. You might like to go to church on Sundays and tithe regularly and he might not see the value in attending church. He might not like sex as often as you do. He might not be as good at sex as you like or need. You may like to travel and he wants to stay in town. He might not be close to his family and envies your relationship with your family.

The list of conflicts could go on and on, but I hope you get the point. Those things might, on the surface, seem like minor things that are not deal-breakers. But if they are important to you, as you get deeper into the relationship, they could weigh on you so heavily that they become major problems.

So, that's where making a relationship last forever starts—with the right mate. That begs the next question: How do you know if you are with the right person?

The precise person for you makes you feel special. He appreciates you; doesn't take you for granted. He's in touch with you enough to be empathetic when you need support and comforting when you need a hug. He's not above being romantic or spontaneous. He's attentive and protective— not jealous or overly protective. He trusts that you honor him at all times and lift up the relationship.

He will be your closest friend, the one you can call on for anything, reveal the most closely guarded feelings to, and count on to be your rock when you are unsteady. And you will be that for him.

Some of the lyrics to my classic song, "Make It Last Forever," go like this:

Let me hear you tell me you love me
Let me hear you say you'll never leave me
Ooh, girl, that would make me feel so right
Let me hear you tell me you want me
Let me hear you say you'll never leave me, baby
Until the morning light . . .

I wrote those words to express the value of sharing your feelings of commitment and devotion to the person in your life. That's a very important part of making your relationship thrive until the end of time—you have to be open to expressing your deepest, most emotional and heartfelt feelings.

Think about it this way: Every time someone you love tells you that he loves you, doesn't that make you melt? Doesn't it feel good? Doesn't it make you smile, if not outwardly, then certainly inside? Those feelings reinforce his love for you and they should inspire you to share similar feelings to your mate.

Those exchanges of emotions, feelings and commitment offer each of you strength to persevere during the inevitable turbulent times. It gives you something to draw on when he gets on your last nerve.

It also helps that you be fair in the things you communicate. In other words, if you are quick to complain about something, you should be as equally quick to compliment. It goes back to making that client feel special.

That's part of the "work" that is involved with making a relationship successful. You hear all the time that "relationships are hard work." Some are more hard work than others. Each requires that commitment to success.

If you go in understanding that an effort has to be made to please your partner—that you cannot just receive without giving back—you stand a better chance of getting out of it what you desire. And if you get out of it what you desire, then you are prone to stay in it longer, prone to stay in it forever.

KEITH'S KEY: Relationships can last forever...with strength, honor and commitment—and the right decision on who works for you. Society brings this pressure or expectation that we grow old with someone. I don't really have a problem with that thinking. But it has to be about *who* that person is and how that person fits into what's important to *me*.

As another of my songs indicates, "There's a right way and a wrong way to love someone." I wrote that song to point out that we cannot just be with someone because they love us or say they love us. They have to love us the right way, the way that makes us feel good and comfortable and right.

The divorce and breakup rates are so high because so many of us decide on the person who loves us the wrong way—or does not even know how to love. We can't be mad at them. They are who they are. It's up to us to determine our own relationship life. I have made choices that when I reflect on them now, I wonder if I fell and bumped my head. The women were good women, good people. But they were not good for me.

And in every case they told me that in their actions not long after getting to know them. So, it fell on me to make a decision on whether to continue dealing with them. Like you or many people you know, I had the idea that I could "fix" that person or deal with the areas that did not really appeal to me.

I should have realized early that you cannot change someone and the little things that bother you will not go away—and that they could add up to something big down the road. I know a lot of people who are in long-term relationships and married who simply are not happy. They are "enduring" or "managing" or "putting up" with the person and the relationship. To me, that's not exactly the way to live.

We all should have healthy, exciting, fun, fulfilling relationships with people who love, respect and honor us. Choosing the right person is a huge part of receiving that.

CHAPTER TWELVE

LONG DISTANCE RELATIONSHIPS *CAN* WORK

I know a woman who said she was done dating guys who did not live in her city. Time and time again, while in New Orleans at the Essence Music Festival or at the NBA All-Star Game in some neutral city, she would meet guys from other locales and begin cross-country romances. They would start strong…but fade fast.

Most of the time the relationship diminished because one or both parties did not possess the stamina to keep things going. One of three things happened: They got disenchanted with not being able to see each other daily, they got distracted by others interested in them that lived nearby, or they could not afford the financial burden required to visit on a regular basis.

All those are legitimate reasons for a long distance relationship to falter. But that does not mean that's the fate of all such relationships. In fact, I know of many cases where the distance was not a problem and even helped the relationships stay together and flourish.

Much of it is a mindset of trust. You first have to exhibit a trust in that person that is unbreakable. Most of us have been in at least one relationship where we either cheated on our mate, or were cheated on. That experience lets us know it can happen, which usually puts us in an uncomfortable place with anyone, but especially when that person is not constantly in our presence.

That's when you have to trust yourself to trust. That's not to encourage you to be silly or blind. But to give the relationship a fair chance, you must give that person the benefit of letting experiences with him influence how you act or think—and not the unfortunate past.

You owe it to yourself to let it go because it surely will prevent you from discovering whether or not what you have is real. Too many people go into long distance relationships so full of suspicion that it is doomed before it could even take flight. If your attitude is upbeat and positive, your chances of making it work in an out-of-state relationship increases a lot.

Why? Because a positive outlook promotes a good mood, meaning you embrace the new interest with enthusiasm and excitement. When you speak to him, you are cheery and alive, smiling and feeling upbeat. That is so important in making the long distance relationship work, even more so than in a traditional relationship.

And why is that? Because when you are in close proximity, being in a blah mood can be overcome simply by someone's presence. If you're connected, you should be able to feel that person's energy, which can either comfort you or bring you some measure of relief from your doldrums.

When you live in one state and your friend lives in another, you have to consciously muffle your ill moods. Not to be fake; that's not what I am saying. It's just that it's important for you to project vibes that will speak to how happy you are in life, as no one enjoys being around or connected to a sourpuss.

In other words, it takes more work to make sure your long distance relationship thrives. The work consists of:

Communication: Like in any relationship, expressing yourself openly and embracing what your mate expresses to you is vital. So many breakdowns in relationships happen because of a lack of communication and/or miscommunication. He said this, but she thought he meant that. And vice versa.

When you communicate effectively, you are in tune with your mate. You hear him. And when you are dating someone who lives a long distance from you, that communication has to be tight. There is no room for a lag in being in contact. A long distance relationship requires more attention than a conventional relationship. And I don't mean just in quantity. I mean especially in quality.

Conversations of substance help build trust and closeness, even across the miles. You might not be able to, or even want to, speak on the phone every day, but when you do talk, it should be meaningful conversations about what's going on in your life and in his life. The convos should include, at times, plans for getting together, talk of the future, expressions of affection for each other. It should never be forced; it should be natural and realistic.

Being away from each other makes it imperative that you really share what's on your mind and heart. That kind of interaction keeps each party attentive and excited about what lies ahead.

Today's technology makes it such that you can communicate daily with no problem. Text messaging can at times be impersonal, but it also can be very effective in conveying your feelings or thoughts at that moment without being intrusive. For instance, you are in the middle of a hectic workday that has you frustrated and tired. Suddenly, you hear your phone chime, indicating you have a text message. You pick up your phone and it's a text message from your long distance friend, saying, *"Just wanted you to know you are on my mind right now. Have a great day."*

Something that would take less than thirty seconds would go a long way. It goes back to what I mentioned earlier in the book—using text messages to your advantage. The distance does not seem as far when you hear from the person you are involved in and they hear from you with some nice words that bring a smile to their face.

I would go so far as to say that you should use text messaging as a valuable tool to keep in touch with your long distance partner. Do not use it in place of talking; don't make it your primary source of communication. But it can be a great supplement.

You should not wish him "Happy Birthday" via text or some other personal occasion that really calls for voice-to-voice communication. And you do not—and should not—offer long, extended thoughts—unless that is what you all grow into. But you should send informative, lighthearted, thoughtful messages that let him know you're thinking of him and that he matters.

In turn, you will receive exactly the same from him. Some people, however, are not fond of text messaging as others. But receiving loving notes certainly can inspire someone to make exceptions.

Once you advance the relationship to intimacy and a true comfort level has been established, the idea of text messages with sexual innuendo is not off-limits. "Sexting," as they call it, can actually add spice to a long distance relationship and help build the anticipation of your next coming together. This is not to condone doing it or to even suggest that you should. These types of correspondences are very personal and something you would not like to fall into the wrong hands. So be very careful and selective about what you say and whom you say it to.

But there is no reason, between two consenting adults who trust each other, that graphic, sensual text messages cannot be shared. Now, we all have heard of people sending graphic photos via cell phones. That's something that I would not recommend. Too often they end up in places the sender would never want.

Additionally, when you're in a long distance relationship, it is important to do some things you might not normally do to keep the interest hot. One way to do that is with mail. These days, we do not go to the mailbox with any excitement. Usually we go with the idea of only collecting bills and/or store coupons. Hardly do we receive something nice from someone. Imagine what it would be like to occasionally receive a handwritten letter in the mail. How would that make you feel? Special, right? And yes, I realize that I have mentioned this a couple of times earlier in the book, but I cannot stress the intimacy of that connection enough.

If you don't feel like putting pen to paper, there are dozens of greeting cards to choose from that can convey what you'd like to convey. Getting one that speaks to your feelings, signing and sending it to your long distance friend every so often would go a long way toward creating a bond.

It is those kinds of actions that help a long distance relationship not only stay afloat, but also thrive. All relationships require great communication and thoughtfulness, but more of it is requirement when you live in one town and the person you are involved with lives in another.

PATIENCE: It is such a great feeling to meet someone you gain a connection with and feel there is realistic potential in building something. Normally, when you live in the same city, you can accelerate the pace of the relation-ship as you see fit through many face-to-face meetings over meals, cocktails, or through sitting together and seeing each other's faces and reactions. But when you live away from each other, those in-person encounters are not nearly as frequent.

That can be very frustrating and even discouraging. But this is where your desire to see it through must be really strong. Patience. As much as you want to pick up the pace, because of the distance, you have to slow down your mind. How you adapt to the approach of being in separate cities will help you control your anxiety.

It's like this: Because you have a life in your city and your friend has one in his, you have to condition your mind that you will not see this person but every so often. So the key thing to do is to make the most out of every opportunity you have together.

No, that is not easy—especially when you really begin to care about your friend. But if you are patient, you can minimize the frustration that comes with infrequent access.

The cliché, "patience is a virtue," really makes sense in any relationship, but most definitely a long distance relationship. It means that if you let things progress naturally and not force the issue, you should get the result you are supposed to get. In a relationship, we do not know what you are "supposed" to get when you meet someone new. But I do know that being patient allows you to see all you should see because you let the truth come into your vision at a moderate, easily identifiable pace. You're able to dissect it clearly because you are not rushed.

If you begin to like someone, your mind tells you to push forward so you can hurry up and get where you think the relationship *should* go. It's only natural. We can see what could be and then we want to get to it. Being patient prevents the quick judgment and potential mistakes. No need to rush anything. Take your time. Relax. Enjoy the courtship, the getting-to-know process. If there is a problem in the whole dating scene, it is the lack of patience. Women, in particular, should be more deliberate, especially when dealing with someone out of town. Rushing into something with someone you do not truly know can lead to something you do not want. Drama.

Planning will help with your patience. Look ahead to times you can reconnect. Look out as far as you can and set a date. You can then begin a countdown in your head—and heart—that will give you something to look forward to. You can never underestimate the value of having something to look forward to in your life.

And get into the planning of the visit. If you are visiting him, go on the Internet and find places you can experience together. Do not take the lead away from him, but find options that might work for you, so you can make suggestions if need be. And when you are the host, make it special for him by planning activities that promote fun. Again, being proactive in what you do will give you something productive to do and look forward to—and help you ease the anxiety of being apart.

UNDERSTANDING: You never know what people are going through. Most people hold back their most private concerns. Many times their problems impact their mood. When you're in a long distance relationship, you have to exhibit understanding like never before.

Being understanding will give the relationship a real chance to grow. There will be times when schedules will conflict or the money will not be there to travel, preventing you from getting together. Instead of letting that frustration mount into something really big, you have to call on understanding to get through it.

Let's say your company Christmas party is on the same weekend as his mother's birthday party. They are in different cities and there is no way he can make it to your event.

As much as you'd like him to be there—to show him off to coworkers and friends and for your own gratification—you have to give way to the fact that he has another obligation that he cannot break. That's being understanding. And if you take an understanding approach, you are less likely to pout about his absence or complain about it.

One of the best rules of thumb to exercise would be to place yourself in his position. When you truly take a look at the situation from your mate's perspective, you are able to get a better understanding of his situation, which helps you in dealing with the dilemma.

Here's another scenario that would require understanding: You want him to visit you on a particular weekend, but he has financial obligations that prevent him from investing the money to get there. If you really like and care about the man, it would be better to be understanding of his plight instead of complaining about it. If you understand that money can be an issue for anyone at any time, then you eliminate the potential for frustration. You can be disappointed—that's a given. But to be frustrated to the point of anger and/or to where you act differently toward him does not serve the relationship well.

Also, because you do not get to witness what his day-to-day life is like on a regular basis, you should not be presumptuous that he should be available every time you expect him to be available to you. Being in a long distance relationship tests you, and that is among the biggest tests—being understanding and not accusing when your instincts tell you to otherwise.

TRUST: None of the above matters if you do not trust the person you are with, especially when you reside in different states. It is easy to let your imagination take you down a dark path. But you will drive yourself crazy—and your friend, too—if you give in to those feelings.

The key to eliminating or minimizing those feelings is to work hard to build trust. Set the example for your mate so he can see, from your behavior, how he should comport himself. In other words, first and foremost, be faithful to him. If you're building a relationship, the last thing you need to do is cloud the situation by having someone on the side, even if you contend there are no emotions involved. The only way to build anything is to do so with a clear mind and by giving your undivided attention to your man of interest.

Secondly, be accessible. Everyone is busy and cannot be available at all times. But it should not be a challenge for him to connect with you over the phone—and vice versa. Be reliable; make him feel like he can count on speaking to you in whatever pattern you all decide works for you. If you agree to speak every other night, be available then. And if you cannot be available, give the man a heads-up that you cannot. The worst thing that can happen is to disappear without a trace and reemerge the next day as if nothing happened. That raises suspicions and chips away at trust.

If you plan to go out with your girlfriends on Friday night, tell him your plans. That's respectful and it gives him some expectation of your activities. Trust is the hardest thing to have in any relationship, but it is virtually impossible to succeed in a long distance relationship without it. So, you have to be particularly communicative to build that trust.

Let's say you told him you would call at ten o'clock. But you did not sleep well the night before and had a particularly long day at work. By ten o'clock, you dozed off on the couch. When you woke up, it was almost midnight. Instead of saying, "Well, it's too late to call him now. I'll call him tomorrow," it is much better to call him at that moment to apologize and let him know that you fell asleep.

Some people may think that is doing too much, but the reality is that in building trust you have to extend yourself in that way. It's doing what is right. You don't want him to think you were out with another man, do you? If you don't, then you should do what is necessary to give him some comfort.

Now, it would be up to him to trust that you are telling him the truth. But if you have been reliable over time, you would have built up enough trust that he would not look at you calling him at midnight as some distrustful act. He would understand and believe that you fell asleep because you had been consistent in your availability to him.

So many people do not understand that trust is complied by the small things as much as the big things. You should make it a rule to do what you say you are going to do. It's a simple thing, but something so many people just cannot do on a consistent level.

Some people think it's being henpecked to be so on point. Some people think they are preventing their mate from being controlling. And some are so distracted or all over the place that they cannot do much of anything close to when they say they will do it.

Those are the same people who are the least trusted. And they wonder why, too. More than that, they complain when you do not do what you say you are going to do.

All it takes is a little caring to be reliable. And being reliable helps your mate trust you. Of course, all of this goes both ways. If your man is consistent about calling you and communicating with you and visiting you, it stands to reason you will trust him more and more.

In a long distance relationship especially, the trust has to be rock-solid. And it will only happen if you and your mate work diligently at building it through consistent behavior.

FIDELITY: All of the above will not matter if either party in a long distance relationship uses the miles as a runway to seeing other people. It seems easy enough to do—the person is not there, giving you free reign to do whatever you please.

But this is actually what patience, understanding, and trust manifests into…fidelity.

If you commit to a monogamous relationship, you have to hold yourself to that by dismissing all the temptation that is bound to come your way with your lover living out of town.

This, of course, will be a challenge. There will be times when there is a concert you'd like to attend, but your partner cannot be there. Do you go with another man who has an interest in you? Or do you bypass the event? The safe play is to go alone, with girlfriends, or not at all. Going out with someone who has an interest in you only gives that person hope he can be more than what he is to you, no matter what you verbalize to him. He will go on your actions, and going out with him says, "I'm interested."

A lot of times we have these people in our lives that we do not have a "relationship" with, but we engage in sex with them. They're like a security blanket, someone to call on to knock the edge off when we need physical contact. When you're in a serious relationship, that person has to be non-existent. It is unfair to your partner to give your body to someone else, even if you believe he'll never find out.

How many times have you had secrets become common knowledge to the one person you did not want to know? What's the saying? All things done in the dark come to light.

Nothing could be worse than disappointing someone you care about—especially over something as simple as temporary gratification. In order to stay the course and be faithful, you have to raise the bar on your discipline and self-respect.

Look at it this way: To be involved in a long distance relationship means you have some serious feelings for this person. Why put something at risk that you see potential in for some bumping and grinding?

The other way to look at it is from your friend's perspective. What if it is you who finds out that *he* is messing around on you? How devastating would that be? If you do not want to feel bad about his indiscretions, you should not want to risk him feeling the same way. That's only fair, right?

KEITH'S KEY: As far as a long distance relationship goes, making it last forever is definitely a four-step process described above. You have to be patient—with him and yourself—and not force the action. Let the relationship grow at a pace that is orderly and not rushed. If you're patient, then you can be understanding and not frustrated at not being able to see your friend whenever you desire to do so. You understand that he might not be available to talk every time you want to talk.

In turn, you build trust through your patience and understanding—and being upfront and honest about your feelings. You do what you say you are going to do and respect him when he does the same thing. Finally, all of that is capped by being faithful. Old boyfriends or sex partners, or new potential men in your life, are completely thrown to the wayside. You fulfill your loneliness with anything other than breaking your commitment to him. If both of you follow these four principles, your relationship has success written all over it.

CHAPTER THIRTEEN

OVERCOMING BROKEN TRUST: IT *CAN* BE DONE

Almost all the relationships that are poisoned are the result of trust being broken. You were either caught with another man, or you caught him with another woman. Sometimes, "caught" does not mean in the act. Sometimes it just means knowing your mate has planned to be with someone else, tried to get with another woman, or has actually been with that person, although you did not witness it.

Of course, this goes both ways. I know of men who were simply devastated to learn their women had stepped out on them. Usually, a woman is far more discreet and calculating than a man. They have a sneakiness that can allow them to do all the dirt they want, but never give any clue that they have.

Men, meanwhile, can be sloppy and careless, many times making it easy for a woman to detect something is going on.

In the end, how you find out there is some shady stuff going on is less important than it is how you recover from it. So often the person who steps out does so not because he did not love the person he was involved with, but because he wanted variety, was curious, didn't think it would matter, couldn't say no, was drunk, didn't think you cared...and on and on.

The way I see it, you cheat because you want to. And you know what? It likely isn't your fault. Now, of course, there are many examples of someone seeking love outside of the relationship because he/she was treated badly. But more times than anyone might imagine, it happens because of no fault of your own. Sometimes, people do messed-up stuff and don't have any real reasons why they did it, either.

Whatever the case, you have found out that your man has been unfaithful. As much as you hate him for this breach of commitment, you still love him.

He claims to want you and will never cheat on you again. What do you do? How do you handle staying with someone that has betrayed you in the most horrific way?

On the other side, you have betrayed your mate, but you do not want to leave. You love him and want him to forgive you and give you another chance. What do you do if he gives you that chance?

This is not an easy fix. A heart has been broken. Trust has been destroyed. Those are the two most difficult breaches to mend in a relationship. And forgiving someone and accepting him back into your life is equally difficult.

There is not a foolproof way to get beyond either. And in some cases, depending on your past, you might not even want to *attempt* to get over the drama; you may just want to move on. I have had to ask forgiveness for being unfaithful, and it was a really hard thing to deal with for a few reasons: One, I let myself down by disappointing someone who expected more out of me. Two, seeing the pain on her face was tough to witness. And three, I knew it would be hard to regain her trust.

I truly was sorry for my indiscretion, and I did all I could do to let her know that. That would be the first step in trying to get beyond it: Humble yourself. If you have wronged someone, you must discard any notion of defending yourself or justifying your actions. That's the last thing your hurting mate wants to hear—you trying to excuse away betraying the person in your life. There could be a period where the hurt mate fires many verbal assaults at you, attacks that are purely emotional and meant to get back at you.

As the person who started the drama, you cannot respond to the attacks. They are emotional outbursts that help the disappointed party get some measure of revenge. You cannot take them personally. You have to stay humble and keep quiet—and apologize profusely and with sincerity.

Many men caught in infidelities do the predictable thing and make grand purchases as a way of expressing their sorrow and asking for forgiveness. And that might—depending on how shallow the woman is—get you back in the door. But it will not matter if you go back to your old ways.

My position on trying to make amends is to do it through words *and* actions. If you are truly sincere, you will not have a problem with either. A woman's instincts are mostly keen, and they surely can tell if you are sincere about your apology and intentions on making amends.

But the only real proof of what someone will do is what someone does!!! And you, as someone examining your mate seeking redemption, have to see what you see and not what you *want* to see. Do you understand that? Let me explain.

Many times, we want something so badly that we ignore clear warning signs. We see issues, but we look beyond them for one reason: We don't want to see them. We want what we want.

It happens all the time. That's why I tell women not to go searching for a man. You put getting a man into your psyche, and he could have all kinds of flaws exposed, but because you told yourself you want him, you dismiss the flaws as something that you can live with—just to fulfill your goal. And when you do that you so often end up getting tired of the flaws you realized existed in the first place.

It would be better to simply live and allow things to happen naturally. Do not force anything. If it doesn't fit, forcing it is only going to put you in an awkward position. If not at that moment, at some point relatively soon.

On the other hand, if you remain even-tempered and patient, the person that comes your way has a better chance of being the person for you. At the very least you will give yourself a true opportunity for honest discovery.

This brings us right back to regaining trust. It is all about being patient and allowing that person to *show* his remorse, his true feelings. Once you do that, you are able to assess with a clear mind and heart if you want to give him a second chance.

From the other side, regaining trust has to be done with equal patience and care. You cannot overwhelm your mate. But you cannot be too passive, either. It's a delicate balance that has to be straddled. But if you are committed to gaining forgiveness, you will, simply, do what it takes. You will not give up.

CHAPTER FOURTEEN

"THE SWEAT HOTEL, APOLOGY HOUR"

As a nationally syndicated radio host, I have had brief conversations with countless listeners across the country who seek clarity in their relationships and/or decision-making in those unions. I have offered advice freely—sometimes delicately, often harshly and always honestly and with the best intentions on helping.

The callers have come from the more than forty cities where "The Sweat Hotel" is aired. I have enjoyed, and continue to enjoy, the back-and-forth, the sharing, the laughs, the resolutions and the growth. This book could be comprised solely of conversations with my loyal listeners. But we'll dedicate just a few chapters on some relationship dilemmas and my recommendations.

During the "Apology Hour" of "The Sweat Hotel," callers offer their sorrow about their behavior in their relationships. Some issues are quite serious, some a little humorous, all interesting. Here are my responses in trying to help listeners negotiate their concerns:

ON ABUSE: You have to be absolute about this: Abuse should not be tolerated at any point, for any reason. Too often I have heard women make excuses for the man: "He's depressed." "He lost his job and is frustrated." "He didn't mean to do it." "He apologized." "He grew up in a broken home." "He saw his father do that to his mother." "He's not a bad person."

You can offer any excuse you like—there is no justification for staying in a relationship where there is a true threat to your well-being. Don't we all cringe when we read in a newspaper that a husband or boyfriend killed his wife, girlfriend, or even ex-girlfriend or ex-wife? You can bet that, in the majority of those cases, there were clear warning signs that the abuse could escalate to that level.

I recall a case of a woman who said her man took out the ills of the world on her. Bad day at work? He beat her. Family drama? He hit her. Friend did him wrong? He punched her. If you have no control over what happens outside of the house and he's taking it out on you, why should you be there to be his figurative punching bag? What did you do to deserve that? I do not advocate running at every turn. But when your man brings you negative energy that rises to abuse because of frustrations at work, with his family or friends, that is grounds to get to stepping.

One punch becomes two punches, then three, and then something even uglier. Here's the rule of thumb: At the first sign of abuse, run. And don't look back.

But here's the thing: Even more prevalent and potentially damaging as the physical abuse is the mental abuse that men often lay on women. If your man has made it so that you are paranoid about not answering your cell phone every time he calls, he has inflicted a measure of mental abuse on you. You believe he will react negatively to you being unavailable every time he reaches out to you, meaning you live in a constant state of fear of his reaction.

And this is not just about answering the phone. It can be about not being home when he thinks you should be home or about you going out with friends or about your making more money than he does or not having dinner ready when he gets home. No matter what the case, it is unfair to live in fear that his attitude will be determined by you doing whatever it is he puts on you. That's mental abuse, and it is a constant in many of our relationships.

It is as lethal as physical abuse. It wears on you. It tears into your self-esteem. It diminishes your drive. It affects your mood. You are not happy. You take out your unhappiness on your children. You become complacent about your job. You see yourself as less than who you are. You become tired all the time.

All that is because the mental abuse you are enduring. Who needs that? No one. So, while the signs of physical abuse are more readily visible, the impact of mental abuse is just as devastating.

ON DEALING WITH MARRIED MEN: Some things in life are complicated and require a lot of thought and strategy to solve. Other things are as simple as one plus one. When it comes to dealing with married men, ladies, you already know the answer. I get so many calls on "The Sweat Hotel" from women asking advice on how to deal with the married man in their lives. It's easy: RUN!!! And don't look back.

There are a few important things to consider when it comes to this. One, put yourself in the shoes of the wife. You wouldn't want your husband running around with some woman. Understand that your actions with her husband are hurtful—to her and their children, if they have kids. You do not want to be that girl.

Two, realize that the married man is not going anywhere as long as you continue to give your body to him. Why would he if he can have you as he pleases, when he pleases, and still have his married life? You have to understand your value and look at yourself in the mirror with pride. You cannot be proud of yourself as the "jump off" or the "other woman" or the "woman on the side." That's a nasty role that does not shine dignity on who you are as a woman. That alone should be enough for you to understand it is better to be alone than to defile yourself.

I have heard from callers who say they have been in a relationship with a married man for almost twenty years. Maybe I'm silly, but that seems downright crazy to me. I am intentionally using harsh words to hopefully shame you into kicking that married man to the curb, so you can move on with your life. It is immoral and just plain wrong to be caught up in that situation.

Perhaps we really should address how this happens in the first place. What makes you turn to another man when you are married? Has your marriage lost its zeal? Are you no longer attracted to your mate? Are you "paying him back" for cheating on you?

Guess what: None of those reasons are reason enough for you to demean yourself. Whatever your motivation, you have to fight against it. Bottom line: It is not worth it. He is not worth it.

Think about it: If he is low-down enough to cheat on his wife, what does that make him? What does it say about his character? It says he will do anything to get what he wants, including lying to you about his situation and the future of his situation. There is no reason to get caught up in that ugly cycle.

And I don't want to hear about how good the sex is. I'm the first to tell anyone how important sex and passion is to a relationship. But that's to a "relationship," not an affair. There's a big difference.

Here's the thing: This goes for the man, too, who is single and running around with a married woman. You might think you're getting what you want, but you wouldn't want your woman seeing another man. Put yourself in the husband's position and that should be enough to cut it out.

ON PAYBACK: "I confess that I have been sleeping around with someone else. My boyfriend was sleeping around on me first with my best friend. I forgave him. But I don't want to be with him anymore. A woman can take but so much."

Unfortunately, this is a familiar, sad story. When you are hurt, you might say you forgive your man, but that is a heavy burden to bear. For sure, you didn't forget. So, when an opportunity for you presented itself, you jumped at it, reasoning that he cheated on you with your best friend, so you had room to do similar. But here's what it comes down to: Two wrongs do not make up for the hurt and humiliation he put you through when he cheated on you. If you are saying you forgive the man, then truly do that so you can be the woman you are supposed to be in the relationship and not a vengeful woman who is equally wrong and unscrupulous. Do not let someone else's dirty actions bring you down to the gutter. Remain a woman, remain principled, remain righteous. You'll be able to look at yourself in the mirror every day without regret or embarrassment.

ON LETTING GO OF THE EX: So the woman calls in and says she divorced her husband, but they continued to sleep together. Then he got remarried to someone else and she continued to sleep with him. That act turns him into someone else's man. And that makes him off-limits.

And I don't want to hear that nonsense, "He was mine first." He's not yours *now*, meaning he's not yours to do with as you please. There have been many calls when the woman is in tears about the "ex," although he has clearly moved on with a new wife and has expressed no intentions of divorcing or even separating from her. "But I love him," the mistress says.

To which, I say sometimes—too many times—women confuse making love with *being* in love. The guy pleases you and you call yourself in love. Think about it: Would you, in your rational mindset, fall in love with someone who has no respect for his wife, no respect for you, and is totally selfish? Hell, no, you wouldn't. But that is so often the case. Dude was getting what he wanted, turned you out to where you think you're in love, and now you're crying over this sorry predicament you're in.

Listen closely to this because this is important: Love does not hurt. Let me repeat that: Love does not hurt. Love feels great. Love opens you up. Love fulfills you. Love sustains you. But being someone's mistress hardly is about love. You get caught up in a situation you shouldn't be in. We all make mistakes. I've made that mistake. But the bottom line is that you should not involve yourself in a relationship that cannot grow. And there is no way in the world you can grow a relationship with a married man, whether he was your "ex" or not. There is no recourse but to walk away. Whether you are turned out or truly in love, it requires strength to do the right thing. But that's the only way for you to get beyond it—with strength.

ON DEALING WITH INSECURE MEN: There was this woman caller from Montgomery, Alabama. She was concerned because she and her boyfriend—who was thirteen years younger than her—agreed she would not work as she completed studies to get her college degree. This would allow her to get into the work force making substantially more than him; he did not have a college degree.

Months before it was time for her to graduate, he complained that he needed her to quit school and to work because he was struggling making ends meet working at a fast-food restaurant. Was that a fair request?

Well, it was reasonable but not fair. In fact, it smelled of a classic case of a man being threatened or believing he would be less of a man if his woman earned more money than him. That's some pretty weak stuff, but it happens—a lot.

The way for women to negotiate this situation is: Be reassuring to your man. Let him know you are a team and that he is the figurative head of the family. Minimize discussion about salaries. Subtly reinforce how your success combined with his could make you a winning couple. Do not talk down to him or challenge him about finances—unless, of course, there is a severe situation. Encourage and support him to engage in pursuit of promotions or new employment.

The idea is to build his self-esteem so that he is proud of your success and not disappointed that you are the top earner. No, you should not have to go through such efforts with a man. A man should be secure in who he is and what he represents. But sometimes, with some men, their psyche can be fragile or vulnerable. Society implanted the notion that the man is to be the earner, the rock, the leader. And, in theory, there is not much wrong with that. But some men take those ideals to the extreme, and when they do not measure up to them, it can create all kinds of reactions that show up as insecurity, jealousy and even lunacy.

If he is a man of honor, you, as his woman, should not dismiss his feelings or insecurities. It is a delicate balance between reassuring him and placating him, but it's one you have to manage to minimize his discomfort. Above all, don't stop what you have started. Finishing school is only going to help both of you in the long run. And I bet once your healthy checks start to come it, he will ease up on being insecure.

ON INVADING PRIVACY: How many times have we heard this one? I will tell you how many times. *Too* many times. Going through her man's phone, she found a number she was not familiar with and she called it. On the other end was a woman, who proclaimed to be a "friend" of her man's.

Remarkably, the woman was surprised that her man was angry and disappointed and said he did not trust her to be someone who respects his belongings or his privacy. Listen up and listen good: His cell phone is not yours to go through. It's not cool to take those kinds of liberties.

We've all done it. I can't even front—I have gone through a woman's phone before, too. I'm not proud of it, but I did. And that's why I can say it is the wrong thing to do for a couple of reasons. One, it's a serious invasion of privacy. Two, you almost always create drama that blows up into something huge. In my case, I felt guilty about doing something so underhanded—but not so bad that I did not question her about what I saw.

Sometimes you find something that you believe is one thing, but could be something else. But because you have so much doubt, you cannot fathom that your doubt is wrong.

But here's the simple thing: Do not go into someone else's phone. Or e-mail. Just don't do it. Think of it this way: You're only degrading yourself by stooping that low.

When I have had my personal space invaded, I refused to even discuss what the person so-called "discovered." Why should I answer questions about stuff she had no business seeing? Why should I, when she disrespected my property? Bottom line, if you look for something, you will find something— real or imagined.

Sometimes you don't always find what you think you're going to find. Sometimes you find something surprising. ALL the time, you're wrong for searching. To get beyond the argument that inevitably comes with this breach of trust, you must, as the invader of privacy, offer a sincere apology, ask for forgiveness and vow to never do it again. And you must *keep* your vow.

If you have been violated, you must conjure up deep introspection and calm to deal with the situation—and to accept an apology. If you want to stay with that person and move beyond the drama, you have to deal with it head-on. If you decide you want to answer questions about the information, then do so to clear up any questions. If you decide to not address the questions—which is your right—then politely explain that because your privacy was invaded you do not feel the need to say anything.

ON LOVING TWO PEOPLE AT ONCE: "I have two husbands," the woman says. Aside from that being illegal, her problem was that she said she loved both of the men. She was juggling between the two of them; they lived in different cities. And each was a father to her two children. *And* they knew each other.

What a crazy situation, right?

Her question was not crazy, though: Is it possible to love two people at the same time? The answer is yes. I think. Some people say that if you really love one person in a romantic way, truly love him, then you cannot simultaneously love another man the same way at the same time. Their rationale is that when you love someone you truly turn over your heart to that person, leaving no room for someone else to have a part of your heart. And that makes sense.

The thing about love, though, is that it doesn't always make sense. I can speak for myself and say that, in my days of being a swinging bachelor, I had very strong feelings for two women at the same time. I loved them both. I loved different things about each of them, but I did love them both at the same time.

How does this happen? Well, lots of ways. The most prominent way is from having a relationship with someone you grew to love, and there is a breakup for one reason or another. Although you all have split, your feelings of love remain for that person. Eventually, you meet someone else and eventually fall in love. Your love for the first person does not have to fade because you fell in love with the second person.

Meanwhile, while you are with the second man, something happens to bring the first man back into your life. That's when you end up in a quandary: loving two men at once.

The real trick is how you manage this touchy situation, which is not easy because it is not an exact science. In truth, it would be much better to be involved with just one, despite how you might feel about the other. In other words, make a choice.

Carrying along two people—no matter how much you might love each of them—is unfair. It's unfair to them and it's unfair to you, although you might feel like you're getting the most out of this situation. The reality is that even if you love more than one person at the same time, you should be in *one* relationship at a time, no matter how difficult it might seem. Unless you clone yourself, one or both of the people you contend you love will feel the gap and demand more of you. Meanwhile, you would stretch yourself too much while trying to be everything to two men. It stands to reason that you would get worn down in trying to maintain both of them and run the risk of losing both.

ON BEING PATIENT: The caller said she met a man she was "feeling" but a text message to him "sent him the wrong vibe," and the guy then began an aggressive pursuit of her. She wanted him to know she was interested, but she also did not want him to think she was easy.

This is a common concern among women: How soon is too soon for sex? It usually is the woman's burden because, in the end, women determine if and when that significant step will happen. We can debate all week and into next week about what that timeframe should be. Some will say sex should not occur before three months. Others will say six months. And then there is a huge faction of people who say a timeframe should not be put on it, that as an adult, you should go with your feelings—whether that's one day or one year.

I will say this: A man likes it when a woman plays hard to get. Don't throw yourself on a man. I'm really old school about this. Let a man pursue you for a while, show you that he is really interested, that he cares. And over that time you really get to know him and can really determine if you want to advance the relationship to sex.

Listen, it's not playing a game. I would never advocate game-playing. This is about giving yourself a chance to find out whom you are dealing with. And this is really important: If you give yourself and your body to a man too quickly, he almost certainly will put you in a category that you will not be able to escape. What "too soon" is exactly is hard to decipher. But you can rest assured sex of the first night is too soon. The second night as well.

Being quick with sex will give the man the impression that you routinely do so, and there are few men in the world that would be comfortable believing their women are "easy." As a result, as much as the man might have liked you and enjoyed your intimate time, he likely will brand you too loose for him to consider for a serious, long-term relationship. You would be his "jump off," as they say, that woman who is there for sex and good times only, not as his mate in a fulfilling relationship. He might even take you home to mom, but there won't be an open invitation to return.

Sometimes, too many times, a woman gets so eager to snag a guy that she believes jumping in bed with him quickly is giving him what he needs to choose her. It is one serious misconception.

I don't care how attractive she is, if she throws herself on me, I am completely turned off. I cannot get past believing she would throw herself at someone else, which is not a good thought.

Besides that, I love the chase. I like seeing confidence in a woman who genuinely believes she is worthy of being pursued—and not the other way around. A woman minimizes herself in my eyes by being too forward. You do that and a man immediately puts you in an unflattering category, a category you ultimately will not be able to escape. A man who thinks you are too easy will never give you the proper respect.

Think about it: If you make the first move on a man in an aggressive way, why would he believe he should go through a patient process of getting to know you and gaining affection for you? He wouldn't. Rather, he dismisses any thoughts of really trying to build something with you. His mindset immediately shifts to conquering you in bed because you've made him feel like the true getting-to-know process is unnecessary.

In short, be patient and respectful of yourself. Understand that all good things come in time, and if a man waits for you to show your interest in him, make him wait and experience a much better outcome.

ON MAKING TIME FOR YOUR MATE: The caller needed some time with her man. He worked more and more and later and later, so much so that when he finally gained some free time, he was too tired to do anything more than hang around the house.

"I'm trying to be understanding," she said. "But I don't want a man who just wants to sit around the house all the time. I need him to want to spend some time with me, do things with me."

This was a serious dilemma because the man seemed to believe it was acceptable to sit at home—and that his woman should be content with the situation. Well, he was right—to a degree.

What we all have to do in tight situations is take our own ambitions and emotions out of the situation and try to place ourselves in our mate's position. That is not easy to do, but when we can, we are about to see the other person's position with a clearer perspective and have a better understanding of his feelings. Such a vantage point should allow us to be less demanding and more empathetic to the situation.

Maybe, *hopefully*, looking at it from his point of view would allow you to consider that he's putting time into work, to earning a living, and that grants him some leeway. Show him some support, encourage him, let him know you appreciate his efforts and commitment to bringing tangible stuff to the table. Surely, he will respect that you are understanding and supportive. It will make him more likely sacrifice when you share your ideas, and it's important to support him and appreciate him for that.

Now, that does not, by any stretch of the imagination, mean that he should take your kindness and understanding for weaknesses. And you should not let him. You have to figure out a reasonable amount of time before you impose your will on the situation. If, say, two weeks pass and he insists that he's too fatigued to do anything other than come home and crash, you have to—in a respectful and calm voice—let him know that in a relationship, sacrifices have to be made.

Let him know that a relationship is not built or maintained on solely what he wants to do and when he wants to do it. Sometimes, you have to suck it up and pull yourself off the couch to make your mate happy. And when you do that, you do not do it begrudgingly. You do it with at least the appearance of free will—and you do not spend that time out complaining about how tired you are or how you wish you were not there. Go out and have the best time you can, knowing you did something to please your partner. Trust me, that gesture will not go unnoticed—or unrewarded.

ON WANTING HIS CAKE AND COOKIES, TOO: The situation was this: A woman from north Florida was married a year ago. After seven months, the husband said he wanted out. He needed some time away.

So, she asks me if it's okay that she sees him a "couple of times a week," even though he's expressed that he does not want a divorce, but does not want to move back home, either. Translation: They're having sex a couple of times a week.

It's like this: As long as you give him what he wants—your body—then what's his motivation to come back home? By having sex with him two or three times a week, you are enabling him. He believes he can get what he wants and not give you what you desire. It should not be a tit-for-tat situation, but the reality is that you want something significant from him—to come back home and resume the marriage. He seems to want sex. That's a significant imbalance.

As a rule, I do not believe in or recommend ultimatums. They only back someone in a corner, creating a hostile situation that does no one any good. But this is a case where it would be the best route. Before doing so, break down all the reasons on why he should be about getting the family together. Appeal to his sense of fair play and love for you. Then tell him that you cannot participate in a sex-only relationship with him, and if he does not agree to at least begin working on coming together as a family, then you have to move on.

That's never an easy thing to do—to walk away from something or someone you love. But there are times when principle and self-respect are of the foremost importance. If you do not respect yourself, you cannot expect that someone else will respect you.

ON MOVING ON: The caller received a letter from her boyfriend, who was in jail. He wrote to her that she should move on with her life and not wait for him. He faced years behind bars and thought it best that she not wait for him.

Now, I would consider that a magnanimous gesture; the man believes his woman deserves better. That's basically what he's saying. But the woman's response was, "I ain't trying to do that."

She wanted my advice. I was a little confused. The man could have been like so many other brothers in the can—possessive and controlling, trying to manage her from the inside. But he wanted her to be free of his shenanigans and go on with her life. She didn't want to go. So, I told her that the man was looking out for her best interests. He wanted to spare her feelings. Maybe he was going to be incarcerated longer than she knew. Whatever the case, to not pay attention to his words was setting herself up for trouble down the line. Sometimes people tell us what they want us to know through their actions. A guy cancels dates or shows up late for dates or is distracted when you are together…he's telling you that he does not care enough to be punctual, or even keep dates. And instead of listening, you ignore it all because you want what you want.

And sometimes they tell you how they feel in words. This was a simple case, really. Love or not, you have your life to live. What sense does it make to not live it, especially when the man tells you to move on? It comes down to this: She didn't know *how* to move on.

For a variety of reasons, we get engulfed in someone, invest our time and heart and when it blows up, we want to piece it back together. We'd rather spend all the heartache and effort on trying to hold together something that is fractured and contaminated instead of using that energy to repair ourselves and advance our lives. There's a song, "Breaking Up Is Hard To Do." And while that's true, it's even more difficult to move on once a relationship reaches its end.

There's a tendency from men and women to be almost frightened to break free, even when relationships sputter to a crawl. It's like there is something dark and unfamiliar out there after you break up. That's why the caller was reluctant to let go of a man who was in prison—who told her to move on without him.

THE SWEAT HOTEL, CONFESSION HOUR

D uring the "Confession Hour" of my radio show, I allow callers to sort of vent and get their burden off their minds. I am not a psychiatrist, but I do believe it is important for us to rid ourselves of things that weigh us down.

They could be acts or misdeeds that we have not shared with anyone. I am always surprised by some of the things I hear, even after doing it for so many years. It tells me that we are still behaving badly, but also that we desire redemption from those we hurt or disappoint.

Being able to ask for forgiveness is an important element to making your relationship last. Listen, you're going to do something that calls for a confession, and it is when you can make that statement with sincere regret that we can measure growth in who we are.

Now, we cannot continue to make the same mistakes and think a heartfelt confession is going to ease over the repeated misdeeds. We've got to behave ourselves—and I've included myself in this because I make mistakes and I am hardly perfect.

The following sample of "Confession Hour" calls show that I am not alone in my imperfectness.

ON LOVE ON LOCKDOWN: The caller confesses that she's in love with her pen pal, who happens to be in prison. And married. These kinds of scenarios do not shock me anymore. I have learned that people can find love anywhere, at any time and under any circumstances.

It's really about what you do when you find love. In this case, the caller was in a horrible position, a position that she should not embrace. Her pen pal is married. That fact alone makes her ambition of being with him totally improper. Almost as bad is that he had been in jail for seven years. For assault. That gave me reason to believe she could find a better catch. I had nothing against the brother behind bars. The hope always is that inmates are rehabilitated and re-enter society intent on being good citizens and good mates in relationships.

But I never got it when women perfectly able to meet free men instead opt for men that are locked up. It plays into that theory that most women want a little bad boy in their men. Still, this was more than a *little* bad boy. This was a convicted felon in jail for seven years...*and* married. Logically, it made no sense for her to be involved with him.

I am an advocate for love. It's the best thing in the world. But pursuing an inmate who is married is not the thing to do, no matter how much he talks about his marital problems. Men fall back on their issues with their marriage as if that's a justification for cheating. Women, do not fall for it. Get with a man who is yours and yours alone. And make sure he's not in prison, too.

ON CHEATING AS PAYBACK: The woman wanted to "get back" at her man because "he wasn't there" for her. How did she get back at him? By sleeping with his cousin. Not exactly the way to make a relationship grow, right?

And she wondered why her man wanted no part of her after she made that confession? Duh.

To magnify the situation, she said they had been through a lot together, including losing a baby and getting back together after a previous breakup. But instead of doing something mature—like having a heart-to-heart—she decided to violate his trust in a very vile way.

Unfortunately, it is not uncommon for people to try to hurt their mate in this way. It is one hundred percent opposite of what should be done. Keeping it just plain old real, how can giving your body to someone make your mate feel better about you? Does that make any sense?

Attempting to "pay back" or "get back" or make someone jealous through sleeping with someone else only drives the person farther away. You cheapen yourself, break down trust and etch a perception in his mind that he will never look past.

So, what to do, then, to get your mate's attention when you feel things are going South? There are many options, none of which include going to bed with someone else. In fact, this case of sleeping with her man's cousin is particularly low and cutthroat and sad. It is sad that his cousin would betray him in that way. And it is equally sad that she would target his cousin as someone to bed. That out of the way, the much better approach would be to simply have a conversation about your concerns. Everything should begin with conversation.

Be direct and honest about your feelings. But also be mindful that many times people are sensitive to what they perceive as criticism, so choose your words carefully. Do not baby him, but just know that the way you say things can truly impact the response you receive.

I have had to have similar conversations with women in the past. It always went something like, "Is everything okay? I ask because it seems like you're not yourself, like you're distracted or maybe even bored. Whatever the problem is, let me know so we can fix it."

That approach disarms the person because it makes you appear concerned, sympathetic, and you open the thought that it could be your fault for his issues.

The other approach is to do something that you know the person likes to do. Maybe that will put a spark in him. If he likes to go bowling, set up a bowling night. If he likes to go to karaoke, take him to karaoke. It shows that you like what he likes and that you are in tune with him.

Those are much better options than being evil, deceitful and self-degrading.

ON REAL LOVE: I have had callers routinely say, "I love you," to me, but none like a young lady from Detroit. She said, "I have been in love with you since I was fifteen and now I'm thirty-eight. And it's ruining my life. Men I deal with say, 'Why can't you love me?' And I tell them, 'I'm in love with Keith.' It's crazy. How can you love someone who is not even in your life? How can I love something I never had? I listen to your music and I feel connected to you. It's like it's our world."

She caught me off guard with that one. Of course, I was flattered by the love. At the same time, I was alarmed, so much so that I did not give her the advice I should have in that moment. At the time, I just accepted the admiration and moved on to the next caller. What I should have told her was that, while I was glad she was so enamored with me, the reality was that she needed to let go of a fantasy and deal with reality.

In some way, my music and the idea of me touched her to where she felt a very strong sense of connection. But we had never met, meaning what she felt was conjured up by her imagination or what she desired, but not by what she had. She's not the only person to get caught up in someone's image—sadly, many have gone to extreme lengths to show their so-called "love" for celebrities.

At least this person seemed to know that it was not ideal to claim "love" for someone she did not know. But I think all of us have fallen for someone from afar. The important thing to do is to not let that fascination prevent you from embracing the people in front of you that have an interest in you. You very well could be blocking your blessings by focusing on a fantasy instead of reality.

ON FOLLOWING YOUR INSTINCTS: A woman visiting the United States from London confessed that she was considering extending her stay here because she met a man that struck her interest. "He doesn't want me to go," she said. "Should I go? I have been hurt before and I don't think I want it to go any further. I sense there is another woman involved. I questioned him and he's beating around the bush. He doesn't want to say. He changes the subject."

So, what's really the dilemma here? I'll tell you what it is. So many times women are so captured by the idea of love and/or having a man that they ignore even the most obvious signals that tell them to run. There was no reason for this woman to contemplate not going home because of a man she suspected was not on the up-and-up.

I cannot say I am a one hundred percent believer in "women's intuition," but I do believe that we all can sense when we're dealing with someone who is suspect. It's just a matter of if we act on it.

I have met women who were interesting, but something just did not seem right. And when I continued to communicate with them, the questions I had were answered. They had a man or issues or something that I was able to detect but not quite put my finger on right away.

This woman asked the man a direct question about another woman and he avoided answering it. If that does not clue you in that he already has a woman but wants to play with you, then what should?

Usually, the issues come forward pretty quickly. But I decided to not wait until they come out. I decided I would walk as soon as my instinct kicked in and told me I was not comfortable with that particular woman or situation.

I have found the best way to deal with drama is not to deal with it. The mere potential of drama turns me in the other direction. Who needs it? Some women seem to know the situation is shady but stay in it because they actually do not trust their instincts. Not good. Walk away when that feeling comes forward. You likely will be saving yourself some drama.

ON LETTING GO: The female caller was Puerto Rican, in and out of a relationship with an African-American man. They had a son together, but could not hold their relationship together.

Eventually, they went opposite ways and married. But despite being married and despite the families from both sides insisting they stay apart, they got back together and had an affair.

She confessed her role in the infidelity and said she "does not want him back."

She sounded sincere. But it was also obvious that she still harbored feelings for him. That makes breaking away extremely difficult. And because they have a child together, they will be in contact with each other, making it really tough.

But the way to truly let go of someone is to make a clean break. He's married, you're married—that alone should be enough to cut out any fooling around. But in many cases, it is not enough. Lines have to be drawn that never can be crossed. No time alone together. No unnecessary conversations. No "harmless" night out for drinks. No lunches. No nothing.

You have to be this rigid because you are weak to him as someone you love and as the father of your child. Just do not put yourself in a compromising position. You may always carry feelings and desires for him, but as a married woman—and he as a married man—you have to let go the idea that you will ever cross that line with him again.

ON DEALING WITH YOUR "BABY DADDY": She was five months' pregnant when she learned her man was cheating on her. Although hurt and devastated, she remains in love with him, so much so that she wants him back—even though he is in a relationship. Even though he has not committed to returning to her, he does come over for sex at times that is convenient for him.

You tell me what's wrong with this picture? It always makes me shake my head when I hear about a woman's allegiance to the father of her child. I understand that it is a special thing to produce a child. It's a wonderful gift. But sometimes, when the relationship breaks down, you have to be strong enough to advance your life without him.

You are in a life-long relationship as parents of the child, but the focus should be on making that relationship one that is comfortable and beneficial to the kid. Always, the child should be placed first.

Since the man is taken, you should not center your thoughts on getting him back. And you should not think the best way to get him back is through sex whenever he wants it. In so many different scenarios, women believe they can turn a man's thoughts based on sex. Not.

What you end up doing is lessening his view of you. How can he think highly of you if you demean yourself at his whim? He has no reason to change his behavior because you are providing him what he wants, when he wants it.

It is unfortunate that there are so many women in the category of having "baby daddies." But it is incumbent upon them to allow the men to be in the children's lives, however, not to use the child as a pawn in their relationship goals.

You've heard many times a woman threaten to minimize—if not altogether eliminate—visitation rights as a means of getting back at the father for one reason or another. It could be that he has not paid child support as he should. It could be that he would not leave his current woman for you. It could be a number of things. But the reality is that your child needs his father in his/her life. Period.

It is totally selfish to keep your child away from his father because you have beef with him. If he's a drug addict or abusive or a criminal, that's one thing. You have to then use your best judgment. But other than some really dramatic scenario, you should put the child first.

ON DEALING WITH REJECTION: There's something about our makeup that makes it hard for a man to accept rejection. Most of us will try harder when you turn us away. A male caller from Waycross, Georgia said, "I lost my girl at the first of the year. But I want her back. I've been trying hard to get her back. She's No. 1 in my life. But..."

It is hard to say this, but sometimes we have to just let them go when they say they want to be let go. Ego or not, if they truly are done with you, there is nothing you can do to get her back. That's a hard thing to admit, especially for someone who believes he possesses all the qualities a woman should want.

CHAPTER SIXTEEN
MAKE YOUR MATE YOUR BFF

M en have their "boys," the guys they are closest to and who they share intimate details with and hang with in good times and bad. Women have their "girls," who know where the bodies are buried, so to speak. It is a blessing to have someone so close that you can trust and you can use as a sounding board or for advice.

Sometimes, there is this awkward scenario: Your man's closet friend is a woman. Just reading those words make most women queasy. And, truth be told, men feel the same way.

That's a tough relationship to negotiate. No matter what, the woman tends to be jealous and wary that her man is the prey of his BFF. It has been the cause of major grief and broken up many relationships because the men just did not think it was necessary to give up a good friend for no apparent reason. And the same has happened when women refused to push their close male friends aside.

Let me tell you a story: There was this guy whose best friend was a female. The fact that she was a good-looking female with a hot body made it even worse. When he met his girlfriend, he was out with his female best friend. She even pointed out the woman that would become his girlfriend, saying, "She looks like your type. I don't know what kind of person she is, but she has that look you like."

He took her advice and approached the woman, who liked what she saw in the man and engaged in conversation with him. After a few minutes, the three of them enjoyed a fun conversation. He told the new woman that his BFF encouraged him to introduce himself to her.

"Thank you, girl," she said to the man's close female friend. "Good looking out."

The guy and woman exchanged numbers and vowed to get together in a few days. They did—and his female BFF was with him again. And again on the third date. After that, the couple knew they really liked each other and began seeing each other without the BFF. Before long, they were a true couple, happy and excited about their future.

Well, at least the man was. One night, about six weeks later, after a passionate session of lovemaking, the woman told the man, "I gotta be honest; I have a problem with your relationship with (his BFF). I don't trust her."

The man was shocked. He had met her because his friend suggested he approach her. They hung out together, the three of them. They knew each other and even had lunch together without him. She knew of their close bond for more than twenty years.

"Are you serious?" the guy said. "She's been my closest friend since I was a kid. You know her. Why are you uncomfortable with her as my friend?"

The woman had no concrete reason. She talked about a "feeling" and not trusting women in general. But the reality is that a couple of things happened: One, she was intimate with him, taking her feelings to another level. She saw the virtues of the man and believed he was a good catch. So why wouldn't his BFF see him the same as she does? Two, she didn't trust *him*. Why would he *not* try to get with his BFF? She figured that they were equally smart and attractive.

"I know all about her attributes," the man said. "We're super close. But I don't look at her that way. We've never gone there and we're not going there. You see how we are together. There's no sexual tension, no temptation."

That did not make the woman feel better. "Anyone can slip up at any time," she said. "And how do I know you haven't already been together?"

In only a few minutes after making love, the woman sent the man into a borderline rage. "Listen, I just told you that we have not crossed that line," he said. "That should be enough for you right there."

"Well, it isn't," she said.

"Well, that's a problem—for you," he said. "She is my friend—period. And she's gonna stay my friend. Now don't make this about me having to make a choice. That's not fair."

"I'm not comfortable with you and her spending so much time together," she said. "I hear what you're saying. But I know women, too."

The man grew totally impatient. He liked this new woman, but he did not know where it was going to go. His BFF had been there for him in one way or another for two decades. It was an easy choice, if he was forced to make one.

And he was.

"I have male friends and I have stopped being around them because we're in a relationship," she said.

"I didn't ask you to do that," he said. "And, from what I've seen, you weren't nearly as close to them as I am to my friend."

"I'm not trying to be difficult," she said. She was calm, yet direct. "But if we're going to have a relationship, I have to be number one. You can't be that close to another woman."

It was at that point that the man did the right thing: He slowly got out of the bed and got dressed.

"You're leaving?" she asked.

"No need for me to stay," he said. "I like you and I'm glad we met. We're just getting this thing going and you're already making demands. I'm supposed to discard my closest and most loyal friend? You have no idea how we have been there for each other. It would be an insult for me to tell her something so silly. So, you're making me choose. What you don't know is that this is an easy choice."

This or a similar scenario has played out for many of you reading this. How did you handle it?

The bottom line on the issue of you or your mate having a super-duper close friend—be it the opposite sex or not—is one that has to be carefully maneuvered. I understand how important outside relationships are that existed before the new love in your life. But how do you maintain them without offending the man or woman now gaining in importance to you?

There are a few ways to keep the peace and keep both friends happy:

❤ Include your partner in activities and/or conversations with your BFF. The thinking is that the more familiar your new love is with your BFF, the more it will help him gain an appreciation for not only the character of the person but also how important that person is to you.

❤ Do not include your BFF in too many of your experiences with your man. There's already a discomfort there, spoken or unspoken. To try to include your friend in all your activities with your man will raise eyebrows and increase the discomfort.

❤ Realize and accept that being in a serious relationship means you cannot carry on the same type of relationship with your BFF as before. Relationships require your attention and effort, and it sends a bad signal that you are consistently with or communicating with an outside friend.

❤ Be understanding. There will be times, no matter what you do, that your mate will be jealous, envious and even angry that you find comfort in your BFF. Do not get all riled up with him. Be reassuring and patient. All he's looking for is reassurance and patience from you.

❤ Convince your man that no one is closer to you than him, that the real BFF is him. Maybe even come up with another term, like "super-duper closest friend." Let him know you are close to your BFF in a different way, that your love and intimacy takes you with him to a place no one can match, which should be the truth.

For sure, this could be one of the toughest situations to navigate in a relationship. But as you get closer and closer and feel more and more comfortable with your mate, there should be a shift in how close you become, opening up a line of communication that will truly rival that of your long-time BFF. That's not to say you should replace your old, tight friend. It's to say that you could have *two* BFFs.

And that should help the BFF with benefits—your man—feel secure and unthreatened. In the end, a happy couple should be close enough to each other's go-to source for advice, comfort, reflection, admission and expression.

But there's another twist to this situation: You could be the BFF in the middle of someone's relationship. What do you do? How do you handle a change in the relationship of your super-duper close friend?

The answer is simple, really. You understand he is in a relationship and you back off. You let him determine how much time you spend together and how much you talk. You call on him when you need to, but you should be mindful that a late call about something that is not urgent now should wait until the next day. You do not want to appear too dependent or needy to your friend's girlfriend. Yes, you were friends first and, yes, your bond with him is important to you. But that does not mean you function as you have prior to his new relationship situation. After all, he's your friend and you do not want to cause him any issues in his relationship.

KEITH'S KEY: As someone with a BFF, you should not look at having a man in your life as losing a close friend. Look at it as gaining another confidant and someone you can rely on. But you must be cognizant of not alienating your man; there's no doubt he could become jealous of the inside jokes and familiarity you two share. Bring your man into BFF conversations or activities, the idea being the more he learns of him, the less likely he is to be concerned about your relationship with him. And if your man has a BFF, be nice and include the BFF in some events as a get-to-know measure. You'll be surprised at how wonderful having a familiarity with someone calms your anxieties. Of course, be observant but mindful that it's better to have two BFFs than one angry one or not one at all.

Thereare some guys who do not have a lot of interest in foreplay or romance. They do not care about creating a mood or soft music. When it comes down to sex, they'd like to just get it on.

I hope those guys are a minority. Most guys love the anticipation of sex and passion almost as much as actually having it. It should be an experience that can start long before the actual bumping and grinding. Here are some exciting options to try on your man to keep the spiciness in the relationship:

BE DARING. In a crowded elevator, grab his hand and place it on your butt. I guarantee that will draw a smile from your man—and get his mind flowing toward romance when you get home. That kind of initiative excites a man and lets him know that his woman is ready for action. You could also, if sitting across from him at the table, slip off your pumps and place your foot between his legs. Yes, play footsie with your man. It will put him in the same mindset you are in (if he was not there already). You could also wear attire that you would only wear with your man, something that would show off your curves and set the tone for a sexy evening. And then there always is the old reliable: Come to his house in a raincoat and pumps. That's it. Well, maybe you could wear a bra and panties, but not more than that. So, when you take off your jacket, you reveal your sexiness. Any of those moves definitely will get a rise out of your man, pun intended.

BE FUNNY: If you can make your man laugh, you can keep him relaxed. If you can make him laugh and turn him on, well...you're doing a lot right. The grind of work and life can impact anyone's mood, and it is your job to lessen that anxiety for your man. Here's an idea: Let's say you know your man has to get up at seven for work. Set the clock for six. And when it goes off, he likely will say, "Hey, you set the alarm an hour early." And you tell him, "It wasn't a mistake." Give him that look that he knows means you are ready for passion and he will laugh and get it pretty quickly that you intentionally set the alarm an hour early so you can have intimacy before work.

BE IN CONTROL. If you know how you'd like your man to move—how fast or slow, how hard or soft—then let him know. Don't take over, as if you're a drill sergeant, barking orders to a soldier. But if you grab him by the waist and help him create the motion you like, he will be on board. Holding back does nothing. I have heard women say, "I don't want to do too much because he might think I'm out there." Guess what? You're wrong. He wants a sexual partner who is free-spirited and will go for it. Maybe he's watching a football game and you're not into football, but you're at home and letting him enjoy his downtime in front of the TV. Then halftime comes and that's the time for you to put on a show. Model some lingerie. That will get his mind off of football quickly. Or take him by the hand and lead him into the bedroom. Then tell him, "You're about to score." That kind of assertiveness certainly would not draw a penalty from your man.

BE HANDS-ON. A friend told me that his woman got turned on by shaving his bald head. She liked the trust factor involved in allowing her to put a razor on his scalp. She liked the smooth feel of his head in her hands. She liked to see light glisten off his head. There were times when his head did not need shaving, but his woman shaved it anyway—which turned him on. I don't know of a man who would turn down a massage—especially from the woman he loves. As his woman, you have a license to take that massage anywhere you'd like it to go. And while there is always talk about a man rubbing a woman's feet, don't you think your man would react positively to you having him sit back and relieving some of the tension out of his feet? Also, if he has a beard, learn to shave it for him. There is a sensuality about it that is undeniable. He will appreciate the intensity and focus you put into doing in the right way. He will smell your perfume and maybe even feel your breath on his face—surefire turn-ons. At the same time, ask him to apply polish to your nails—after a foot massage. It would be a turn-on to him while, at the same time, he provides you with something you need. What better combination?

BE AN EXHIBITIONIST. No, I don't mean parading around nude in public so strangers can stare. I mean, it's pretty sexy when a woman strips for her man, slowly and seductively undressing while looking into her man's eyes, blowing him kisses. He will have to show great patience to let you finish, as I'm sure he'll be tempted to pull the rest of your clothes off at some point. He will also show great appreciation when he gets his hands on you. Then there is always the option of slipping off your panties at dinner and *discreetly* sliding them across the table. You can bet that would get his blood flowing—and it'd make you feel sexy, too. And do not forget about a simple kiss. Well, not a simple one. Maybe you are alone on an elevator and you just pull him close to you, get on your tippy toes and plant a strong, passionate kiss on him, so long that when the elevator opens, you are seen by whomever is standing there. You'll be excited in more than one way.

BE ROMANTIC. Sure, you have seen it on television or in the movies, but it works. Leave a trail of rose petals from the living room to your bedroom. Layer the bed petals, making it inviting for him to enter. Play some romantic music—not too loud, but not so low, either. Burn candles—scented, preferably. Create a pleasure palace in your home that the king cannot resist. Be the sexy queen/diva that desires his touch. Work and kids can be overwhelming, but do not let those conditions rule. You could also use those rose petals in the bathtub. Bathing together is as sexual and sensual as you can get. Adding rose petals and some candles and music makes it an experience. Once every two weeks or so, close your bedroom door, blocking off you and your husband from the rest of the world. Bring champagne glasses with you and sip the bubbly with your man, all the while telling him how important he is to you, how much you love him, how happy you are in your relationship. By the time the bottle is finished—*if* you get to finish it—he will feel like the special man that he is to you.

BE AN ACTOR. I don't mean faking anything. I mean role-play. It's an ancient game, but it can be fun and very flirty, helping to set a mood of passion. The one that is fun to play is as if you're meeting for the first time on a blind date. It gives you a chance to be funny and clever and very flirtatious. Your man might think it is silly at first. But once he gets into it, he will abandon all his inhibitions and really get into being bold to this exciting new "stranger." You can take the conversation anywhere, but especially places you would not normally take it. You'll end up learning all kinds of things about him that you never expected, things he never shared with you in a normal setting. You can bet sex will be a big part of the conversation. You will get excited about the back-and-forth. And he will, too. And you can rest assured that when you get home that night, the two "strangers" will have a memorable night of passion.

BE A DANCER. Even the stiffest man cannot resist dancing with his woman. Play music that you know he likes, dim the lights some and grab his hand. Make your living room—or, better yet—your bedroom a private dance floor. Show him your sexiness through your movements—push up against him, tease him—and you can bet he will follow suit. Whether it is an uptempo song like "Make You Sweat" or something soothing and sensual like "Make It Last Forever," show your energy and vibrancy. Show that you are into him. Show your passion. He will definitely appreciate it. And when really feeling frisky, step outside of the box and be that exotic dancer, especially if he's a man who enjoys going to strip clubs. There's nothing wrong with you being his private dancer, giving your man lap dances and arousing him with your moves. Do some of the moves you do in private, moves you have been hesitant to execute. Give him an image that you are a fantasy that is his and his alone. And maybe he'll throw dollars at your feet.

BE PLAYFUL. Let's say you are at an event. It's semi-formal and folks are a little stiff because they are dressed up. When no one is looking, grab your man's butt and squeeze it. It will make him feel uncomfortable at first, but you can bet your action sparked something in him to do the same thing to you. And before you know it, you all are laughing and feeling up each other the rest of the night. And you're having more fun that anyone else there. But that playfulness does not have to be limited to events. You could be walking down the street and decide to smack him on the butt. Not a smack like a punishment, but a seductive smack. He will know the difference. And, again, he will follow suit and you'll have to run to get away from being smacked on your butt. But you will be laughing as you run, and he will be laughing as he chases you. That playful gesture surely will promote a happy demeanor, which will put you both in a fun mood. And fun moods lead to all kinds of good things.

BE A DIVA. A diva is strong and sexy and secure and knows what she wants. That turns a man on. So, while at the movies or at dinner with friends, lean over and whisper into his ear: "I want you to #$@ me tonight." His eyes will grow big and a smile will crease his face. You can bet on that. And whatever you are doing, no matter what it is, all he'll be thinking about is getting you back home and to bed. Or, if he has his own office on his job, surprise him with lunch, with you as the lunch. Lock the door behind you and give your man an afternoon delight that will make it hard for him to focus on work the rest of the afternoon. That's a diva power move. But if you cannot make the office run, when he comes home for dinner one evening, serve yourself up as the main course. Wear a sexy dress or outfit that is so hot he will have trouble focusing on his meal. Send him to the bathroom to wash his hands. When he returns, pull the chair back for him to sit down. Pour him his favorite beverage. Then deliver the dishes one by one, seductively brushing up against him as you deliver each course. Sit across from him and tease him with the way you consume each bite off of your fork. When he asks, "What's this about?" Tell him, "It's about you being my man." Talk about a turn-on. If you make it through the meal, you surely will be the dessert.

BE UNPREDICTABLE. Hardly anyone wants someone who barely ventures from her routine. It is okay to be stable, but not good to be predictable. What being unpredictable comes down to is having a desire to touch your man in some way and then being creative about doing it. There are aggressive methods like pole dancing for him and then there are subtle ways that would be equally appreciated. For instance, a card with a loving message sent to his job would surely make him smile. Receiving mail in these days of high technology is rare. And that's what makes sending something through the postal system so dynamic. He never would expect it. If getting a stamp and dropping it at the post office is too much to ask, then rely on technology. Send him a text message the morning after a beautiful evening and let him know how wonderful it was. Take a cute photo and send it to his cell phone. If you have the capabilities, create a short video letting him know you had something really special waiting for him when he got home. Think that would not give him reason to leave work early—or, at the very least, head directly home after work? Or, just to be nice and give him something to think about, deliver him lunch at work. Dress cute and sexy and drop it off to him and leave. He'll be left there with the memory of how hot you looked and will be eager to get to you at the end of the workday. And, of course, a text message saying simply, "I love you," almost always will come at the point in his day where he needs some reassuring words.

BE COMPLIMENTARY. Yes, women need reassurances and words that make you feel good. And men should always offer them. It's part of being a man, as far as I'm concerned. But you'd better know that a man needs compliments, too. It does not matter how self-assured he appears and how disinterested he might respond to the praise. It matters. He might not need the praise often, but he would love to hear, "Baby, I love you in those jeans." Or, "When I see you in a suit, it gets me excited." Or, "Do you know you're a good-looking man?" So many times women are so caught up into receiving a man's praise and affirmation that they have no concept of delivering the same to him. And here's the thing: If you're not doing it, you can bet another woman is. At work, at the grocery store, at the bar, someone is noticing your man. It makes no sense for him to not receive praise from his woman, but garner it from others. After a while—a *short* while—it will make him wonder if he's appreciated by the woman he wants to value him. And the compliment does not have to be about the physical. You could tell him, "Honey, I really like the way you handled that situation with our son's teacher." Or, "I'm really proud of the father you are." Or, "Thanks for being there for me when I was under the weather." The simple things in life matter so much. And it's a shame that so many of us do not know that.

BE SEXY. The world is cruel and busy and with a job, kids, family—and other unpredictable stuff. It is easy to get lost in all that. But you should not. You cannot. Do not lose yourself in the madness of the day-to-day life. You caught his eye with your sexiness. That's how you *keep* his eye. The energy you once had might not be there anymore—that's what a job, and especially kids, can do to you. But your man is your anchor, and, while he loves you no matter what, he loves a sexy you. So give it to him. Get your hair done. Manicure, pedicure—musts. You don't have to look like Beyoncé every day. Shoot, Beyoncé doesn't look like Beyoncé every day. But there should be commitment to being beautiful, to being appealing, to not let yourself go. And remember this: Sexiness also is about an attitude, a confidence, a sassiness. It can show in the way you walk, the way you look at him, the way you talk to him. I guarantee you that while your man may not say it, he lives for the sexiness in you. When you come home from work in your pumps, instead of kicking them off immediately, strut around the house for your man for a few minutes. Let him see you at your best, or close to it. And when you want to flaunt that sexy lingerie, throw on some pumps for a few minutes. That is what captured his imagination at the start and it is what will hold him.

BE SNEAKY. Not "cheating sneaky," but "surprise-him" sneaky. For instance, if he has a daily planner, get a hold of it and on a day you'd like to have fun with your mate, put in "Hotness @ 9 pm, our bedroom." When he discovers it, he will smile and he will be ready for that date. If he received a promotion on his job, it would be nice of you to invite him to drinks at a spot he might like or a new place as a celebration and surprise him by having a few of your good friends meet you to join in honoring him. It does not have to be something big, just something that shows how proud you are of him and how thoughtful you are.

BE CREATIVE. How about this: Buy him a gift certificate to Victoria's Secret and tell him you want to go shopping. Let him pick out whatever he wants to see you wear. And do not resist his selections, even if it might be something you would not pick for yourself. Remember, it's about him, not you. He will be turned on—and turned out. Personalized gifts are always special and show your creativity. Perhaps there is a collection of songs you all have enjoyed over a period of time. Take the time to burn a CD with a playlist only of those songs that you all enjoy together—or a group of songs that translate your love story.

KEITH'S KEY: Be all you can be. There should be no limits to how you express yourself to your man. The bottom line is this: Keeping things going in a relationship is serious business. It takes thought and effort to make it go. It takes thought and effort from both sides. But if you lead the way, you can bet your man will follow. The idea is to have both sides commit to being that extra special person for each other all the time. You do it enough, it will be come habit, a way of life. And that's what you want.

CHAPTER EIGHTEEN

CAN YOU RECOGNIZE HEALTHY LOVE?

About the best example I can give of an ideal couple is my perception of the relationship between President of the United States, Barack Obama, and his wife, First Lady Michelle. From afar, they appear to have the kind of loving relationship that we all should aspire to achieve.

I could be wrong—I am not in The White House with them—but they, at the very least, give the impression of a couple in love. They hold hands. They look into each other's eyes. They show outward affection. They smile at each other.

Those are the tenets of a healthy relationship. A healthy relationship *looks* like a healthy relationship—in private and public. I think in a lot of cases—too many cases—we were around dysfunctional relationships, and we thought they were "normal."

Well, the fact is, they were not "normal." It was not normal for the father to be absent from the house, or for the single mother to have men in and out of her house (and bed). It was not normal that, if both parents were in the house, they hardly displayed any affection in front of their children.

It was not normal that they argued loudly and regularly—or, worse yet, engaged in physical abuse. We are a product of our upbringing, and it sometimes comes through that if we did not see or be around healthy relationships when we were younger, we just cannot identify them when we are old enough to have them.

And so, if you do not know what a healthy relationship looks like, how can you participate in one? Sometimes, we have something in us that helps us overcome not having seen a strong, healthy relationship and yet we have been a part of them. That's called learning from the bad experiences we sometimes have. Sometimes, we learn what *not* to do from experiences that were not positive. There's an intuition on how things should be and we follow it.

When I was young and just really getting on the dating scene, I used to see couples out on dates holding hands. And I would think: "What's that about? They're walking together. Why the need to hold hands?"

I have not been the most outwardly affectionate guy in public with the women I have been involved with. It wasn't until later in life that I realized holding your woman's hand is a strong show of affection. It's comforting. It also makes her feel protected.

If you are out at dinner, smiling and flirting with your mate shows an emotional connection, as does hugging, sitting next to each other instead of across the table, kissing. These are all signs that exhibit signs of a healthy relationship.

So, what is a healthy relationship? For my money, a healthy relationship is one that is marked with open conversation and expression of feelings, honesty, passion, commitment, sacrifice and love. There are other elements involved, but those are the core pieces.

If you have that, anyone in your presence should know that, should feel it, sense it. People should be able to detect it because the health of your relationship will bubble over, like lava from a volcano.

I have a friend who is in love with his wife. By everything I have witnessed with them, they have a very vibrant and healthy relationship. They love each other and talk through any conflicts. And when they are out, he holds her hand and she looks up and smiles at him and he smiles back. They hug and kiss and they are not ashamed for others to see the affection they have for each other.

I must keep it real: Sometimes I used to feel like I didn't even want to be around them. I would be with this woman who was cool, and who I even liked or cared about. But while we might have been trying to build a healthy relationship, my friends already had one. Their healthy relationship was great for me to see; it showed me how I should behave when I had that kind of healthy bond.

The lesson in this is that there are examples out there for us to emulate, even beyond President Obama and the First Lady. Just go out one night and watch couples and how they interact with each other, how affectionate they are.

If you recall the movie *Jerry McGuire*, the characters portrayed by Cuba Gooding Jr. and Regina King were deeply in love. I appreciated the movie because it showed a truly healthy relationship among a young black couple. They were extremely touchy-feely and loving toward each other. Their healthy relationship played out in public as much as it did in private because it was real.

I'm sure someone is saying, "That was a movie, not real life." And my response to that is, while it was indeed a movie, it still represented what a healthy relationship should look like. A lot of people got out of that movie how football agents undercut each other and other lessons. For me, my biggest and lasting take away from the movie was how beautiful and healthy their relationship was. Their outward affection was so strong in one scene that Tom Cruise and Renée Zellweger were forced to at least attempt to be affectionate toward each other because Cuba and Regina were so powerfully affectionate.

Sure, Hollywood contributed to their actions, but, that aside, you should get the point that when you are in a healthy relationship, you will find yourself holding your mate's hand, hugging him without provocation and generally showing your love and emotional connection through affection.

At the same time, you can easily detect a couple that is in an unhealthy relationship, or at least disengaged. You see it all the time. Those are the couples that you see out at dinner who sit across from each other and spend most of the time looking down at their cell phones, checking e-mails, sending text messages or even playing games.

You can't tell me they are in a healthy relationship when that happens. I have seen a family out—husband, wife, two kids—and everyone is at the table on their cell phones. No conversation. No laughter. They all are engrossed in their little devices. So, if a kid sees his parents do that and not engage each other at dinner, why would he/she think something is wrong with it when they start dating? Again, we are a product of our upbringing, in most cases.

I was one of those people that thought it was okay to check messages and send texts while on a date. It took a smart woman to say to me, "This is crazy. We're out at the dinner table and you can't give me your undivided attention?"

It was then that we made a pact—no cell phones while we were out and supposed to be enjoying each other. It was a tough habit to break. But I understood her position and was able to give her the attention you're supposed to give someone when you're dining together.

This actually leads me to another question: Is chivalry dead? Everywhere I go, I hear stories of women who have not experienced a man who has his chivalry game on. Helping a woman out of the car, holding the door for her, walking on the outside down the street...those efforts should not be an effort. They should be natural gestures that a man executes because you're with a woman and that's what a woman deserves.

Well, if you're not receiving chivalry from a man, it's your fault. It's a shame that many men either do not know how to be a gentleman or do not care to be one. But as the woman, you have to sometimes demand what you deserve. You don't have to be crazy with it; that would not be effective.

However, you can easily make your point. For instance, you all are walking toward a door to exit a building. Instead of opening the door, stand there and wait for him to do so. After a few seconds, he will get the picture. Same thing with the car door. No way a woman should ever have to stand there while a man walks around the car and gets in, leaving the woman to open the car door for herself. No way!!! But do as I mentioned before—stand there until it strikes him that he needs to do his gentlemanly deed.

These acts are simple but important. As the woman, you have to demand the utmost respect, which includes the opening of doors, helping you with your jacket, assisting you out of the car. The man who does not know this is a man who needs to be educated. Sometimes, you find men who will tell other men how they should comport themselves. But really, this is a job for women—being around men who have no notion to be chivalrous when it calls for it. I contend, even, that if young girls told young boys who wear their pants hanging off their butts that they would not date them until they wore pants the way they were made to be worn, you'd see a significant shift. That's the power that women have.

Why do you think so many guys do things they do not want to do? To keep the peace. A woman's power cannot be underestimated and her wrath cannot be overstated. So, quite often men give in rather than face those consequences.

KEITH'S KEY: First of all, the goal should be to identify a healthy relationship. Hopefully, you can look at your own as a shining example. If not, the Obamas are a prime example. A healthy relationship translates into a healthy life, one of fulfillment and peace. If you have not experienced a healthy relationship and haven't even seen one, there is still hope. Observe the unhealthy relationships and do the opposite of what you see—a classic case of learning from the bad as well as the good. Seriously, though, functioning in a healthy relationship promotes affection and connection—two elements that serve a strong purpose in a relationship that thrives. Also, demand that your man be a gentleman. Some women are so used to doing for themselves that they bail out the ungentlemanly men by opening their own doors, putting on their coats, etc. If that is what you want for yourself, go for it. But if you want to be treated like a woman should be treated, subtly point it out.

CHAPTER NINETEEN

BY THE NUMBERS—FIVE WAYS TO MAKE INTIMACY LAST FOREVER

1) TOUCHY-FEELY: I have been as guilty as anyone of getting settled in a relationship and then letting the relationship glide wherever it goes. That's not a good look. In fact, it's a bad look.

It is not hard to get away from the things that made you successful. It's like a basketball game. One team might share the ball with each other unselfishly and build a nice lead against its opponent. Then, all of a sudden, the winning team loses its lead because the players stopped doing the one thing that helped get them the lead, which was sharing the ball. They abandoned their strength.

The same thing can happen in relationships. You get comfortable, complacent, and all of a sudden instead of winning, you're losing.

It is easy to forget about the little things that make such a huge difference in a relationship. Things like giving compliments and even holding hands. You want your man to feel good—and vice versa? Tell him how good he looks, how good he smells, how protected you feel around him, how proud you are of him.

If you don't think that would make a man feel good about you—and what he is to you—then you're badly mistaken. Those reassuring words are golden. They help your man stick his chest out and feel good about himself. We all know women generally feed off of a man telling her that she's beautiful and that she looks great in that outfit, that she smells good.

Well, guess what? Men need the same thing. You feed his ego and quench his need for being appreciated, and you will have a man who is engaged and excited and all about romance.

It is the same with physical contact. Some men—the gruff and less-than-affectionate type—might not be so much into holding hands. But maybe they are into being kissed softly on the face by a woman. That would break down even the most stringent man. And it is highly likely that when you first started dating that he took a kiss on the face as something wonderful and special. Do not lose that by not doing so after you get comfortable with each other.

Trust me, a kiss and hug or quick shoulder massage at the conclusion of the day is so much more warming and romantic than asking him to take out the garbage. I'm just saying.

There has been research done to support the idea that physical affection has a powerful impact. There is a chemical in our bodies called oxytocin that is raised in the man and woman with a warm touch. The University of North Carolina researchers call it the "cuddle" hormone, which gets together with other hormones that, together, bring peace and calm and diminishes the stress level.

And we all know that when the stress level is reduced, we feel so much better, like we can do anything. That's a good place to be.

Another study indicated that reaching over and holding your partner's hand during an argument would actually increase your partner's trust in your position—and might even help sway him to agree with your points.

I bet you didn't know this, but we actually crave touch at birth. A newborn's naked body is placed on the bare chest of his/her mother, a skin-to-skin contact that facilitates the mother-child bond. The importance of that never leaves us. So, to keep that interest and connection with you that you desire, hug your man, kiss him, hold his hand, rub his shoulders—those physical acts show him you care. And they impact him physically, too.

2. MAKE EACH OTHER LAUGH: I love to laugh. I love to laugh so much that my friends call me crazy because I'm always telling jokes or saying something that will make them laugh. I do it because I am naturally funny, but also because it feels good to laugh.

Doesn't it?

There are times in a relationship, tense times, that can only be loosened up with laughter. Doctors and researchers talk about the physical aspects of what smiling and laughing can do for you, and I agree with it.

But I'm talking about how it makes you feel inside. You get happy. And when you can laugh with your man, it makes you feel closer to him. You have to be able to laugh and joke. Your man should be your friend and laughing together should be a part of what you do as a couple.

The amount of laughing you do together will tell you if you should be together. If you're not laughing a lot, you probably are with someone you do not really like.

Think about it: You like this guy, but there are infrequent laugh-together moments. Then, you go to work and there's a guy giving you attention, being nice to you and making you laugh. Almost automatically you will be drawn closer to him because he's making you feel good with his personality when your man isn't. And you know what's next, right? You're setting yourself up for cheating because you feel good about this other man.

I will take it so far as to say that if you don't have consistent laughter in your relationship, you don't have much. That's how important it is to me.

It's almost like a second language. Sometimes, if you are connected and have laughter in your relationship life, you both can burst into laughter just by looking at each other, confusing those around you. You have private jokes or you know something you see will amuse your mate because you have laughed together so much that you are in tune with her sense of humor.

No matter how much fun and laughter you have, eventually you will have relationship storms that you have to endure. Some will be significant, some smaller but just as important. Because you have developed a friendship and have laughed together in abundance, you have laughter and fun to draw from to give you some balance.

Some things can be laughed off, but only if you have a culture of laughter in your relationship.

Of course, not everyone is naturally funny. But that does not mean you cannot be funny at times. Search the Internet for jokes that you can remember and share with your man to make him laugh—and to show that you are not serious all the time and that you appreciate laughter. Also, at times when you decide to stay in for a movie, suggest a comedy that will keep the mood light and fun. Probably nothing works as well as going to a comedy show. An hour's worth of laughing surely promotes a good, lively mood.

On top of that, do not be afraid to laugh at yourself. When you do something silly or awkward, do not take it personally when he jokes about your missteps. Laugh with him. Add a joke to magnify his point. Guys can get along so well because, while they care about each other, they can spend hours on top of hours "joning" or talking about each other. The laughter can be uproarious and loud, but it's really about the bond that comes with shared laughter.

So, tell a joke about him. Since you know him, you should know what he would find funny. Play to that. In other words, do whatever it takes to find or create laughter as often as possible. It is extremely healthy to a relationship.

3. BE A CHEERLEADER: There should be no bigger supporter of your man than YOU. He should feel that you are the legs that keep him upright. No matter the dilemma, the situation, the controversy, you have his back. Period.

I had a woman one time who was the epitome of support. She was my cheerleader in every sense, in every case. She even liked the football team I like because it was my team. She liked every song I ever made. She dismissed my critics as "haters" and, although she was the ultimate woman, I believed she would go to blows to support me if pushed. That kind of support carries a lot of weight.

It can be a tough world out there. Sometimes it can be so rough that your man's confidence can be shaken through the knocks that come with working and trying to make a living. It's your job to make him feel like he's a giant, a king, someone who will conquer all.

Despite a man's strength, he needs the reassurance of the woman in his life. This is different from the physical affection we talked about earlier. This is about being there and telling him how proud you are of the man that he is. Reinforcement goes a long way. He, of course, has to do the same for you. That's what makes a relationship thrive: openly sharing and supporting.

And it helps to be direct and speak to exact strengths in him. A man's self-confidence is critical to his strong existence. In some ways, he's like a kid that has to be fueled with encouragement to keep pushing forward.

This is not about false credit or fake support. I'm not about that. This is about acknowledging those things he does that could go unnoticed. Many times things are handled and no one says anything. They are done because they need to be done and not for recognition. But you should give it anyway.

It could be how he handled a touchy situation at a restaurant. It could be how he put in extra hours on the job to make sure you all had extra vacation money. It could be how he dealt with your son on a school matter. Almost anything could merit your cheerleading.

Now, here's something really, REALLY important: Men focus so much on making you feel good by complimenting you on how nice you look. It's a good idea to let him know that he's sexy or that you noticed he got a haircut or a new shirt. A mutual boosting of self-confidence only adds comfort and security to the relationship. And that's what we all should seek.

4. PICK YOUR ARGUMENT SPOTS: You can try all you like, put all the effort into it you have, but you will get into arguments with your mate. I don't care how sweet and kind and thoughtful and whatever you are, he will get on your nerves about something at some point. Or you will disagree on something—and probably a lot.

That's not the hard part. The hard part is realizing you should not engage in a "fight" over *every* issue. You battle over every concern and you'll not only run him away, but you'll run yourself ragged. And why do that?

So, you have to be selective about what you commit to addressing—or, better yet, how you deal with issues. It is not healthy go to around with issues banging around in your head. It will eat at your stomach and build up to something that could be volatile when it finally comes out.

A better course would be to address concerns, not battle through them. If every issue is a battle, there likely will eventually be a casualty. And that casualty would be the relationship. So, do not hold in stuff that bothers you to "keep the peace."

Talk about what's out there—and encourage him to do the same. You don't feel right when you've got stuff hanging over your head. Some people can fake it like it's all right. But it cannot last. It will eventually impact your spirits and can even hurt your health. Seriously.

So, understand that you do not have to agree on everything. You can politely and respectfully disagree. Talking it out will prevent a build-up of animosity and potential explosion that could come with holding everything in and not expressing your feelings.

The thing about disagreeing is that it really affirms that you are both individuals in the relationship. You do not have to have identical positions on every subject and you don't have to agree when there's a disagreement. That's not to say you shouldn't ever compromise, but you shouldn't sacrifice what makes you the person you are.

Understand that fighting does not mean you are not a happy couple. It means you're a normal couple. It's all in how you address the issues that arise.

5. HAVE COMMON DREAMS: Two of the often-overlooked ways to cause strife in your relationship are to 1) not support your partner's professional and/or personal ambitions and 2) not having common family goals.

It would be silly to be in a relationship unless you had high hopes for it.

I should not even have to write that, but you'd be surprised at the number of people who are in "relationships" that have no direction, nor destination.

What would be the point of committing to someone unless you have high hopes for your future together? That doesn't mean your relationship is going to be the end-all, be all. I have had relationships with women that I could see great things in the future with, and we worked toward them. It might not have worked out as originally thought, but the point is we had a place we wanted to get, which means we weren't just playing around. We had dreams.

On the opposite side, many times, people fall into a boring routine because they lost what being in a relationship really means or what it is about. If you or your mate have drifted into a place where you are merely existing, with no defined ambition, it is then when you have to reel things back in by identifying common goals.

It's like this: When you were dating, you likely talked optimistically about the future, giving the impression of wanting to build together. That kind of hopefulness and collaboration must continue throughout the relationship. If you lose that, you lose something your relationship cannot afford to lose: hope.

It also means a lot that you have your personal dreams supported—and support his. Say for instance, that you want to lose weight and decide to change your eating habits. You would want and need your partner to encourage you along the way on that journey. And vice versa.

Let's say your man decides—after much thought and research—that he wants to fulfill a lifelong dream of opening a barbershop. You knew how important this was to him. He had the resources to make it happen. It would take his joy of fulfilling the dream to another level if he had your support and assistance.

Nurture these dreams both for yourself and your partner. Having something to aim for keeps you moving forward and gives you a break from the everyday monotony of working, eating, and sleeping. A relationship is a journey—where do you want it to take you?

There was an iconic actor long ago named James Dean, who once said something that really makes sense: "Dream as if you'll live forever; live as if you'll die today."

In other words, life is too short to live it in drama. With relationships, there will be problems. But if you love your mate and believe you are where you belong, you have to work through your issues instead of letting them drag on. How do you do that? Here are some principles to consider:

PUT YOURSELF SECOND WITHOUT DENYING YOUR NEEDS. Sound tricky? Not really. This is actually about being connected to your mate through your actions more so than your words.

Here's an example: I know a guy who said his ex-girlfriend could not say, with certainty, what his favorite food was or even his favorite hobby. She just did not have a need to be connected in that way.

Everything was about her. As long as he knew what her favorite food and hobbies were, she was fine. Well, what does that say about what she really feels about him? Not much.

Here's another example: There's a writer I know who was in a long-term relationship with this woman. He was totally in tune to her, her needs, her desires, her ambitions and contributed to all those elements on a consistent basis in one way or another. It might have been to his detriment that he did not ask much of her, other than fidelity and no drama.

But it struck him one day a few years into their relationship that all of her friends and many other people she knew read his books, but his woman did not read them. He pointed out this injustice to her several times, and she never acted on it. She said, "I'm gonna read it," and "I'm gonna surprise you," but did nothing. At the same time, he had immersed himself into her life, helping her start her business, assisting her in getting her new home together, and even aiding her family in various projects.

Rightfully, he became bitter that she did not think enough of him to make time to read his books. It was totally selfish on her part and it was part of the reason their relationship failed. It was a one-sided relationship, which are always doomed to fail.

Those examples show women who believe the world revolves around them. That would be okay if it actually did revolve around them. Or it might even be okay if they were single. But in a relationship, you have to be about your mate. You should know your mate's likes and dislikes, and you should be supportive of your mate in ways that show you care and that you are truly connected.

RELATIONSHIP STAGES: Like most everything else in life, there are stages to a relationship. If you spend enough time to nurture it, you should experience at least three phases that you will have to master to keep the union going strong.

In order, those relationship stages are: building a romance; enduring conflict; and making a commitment.

Building a romance is really what meeting someone is all about. Let's be real about it. You are looking for the attraction and the connection that will bring you closer together to eventually get to romance.

We all want and need romance. When you are in a relationship or meet someone with the potential for a relationship, there has to be a conscious effort to build toward intimacy.

These days, when I man does simple things that were customary in the past—things he is *supposed* to do—he is lauded as someone deserving of credit. Above all, this early stage should be about fun and laughter and getting to a place where there is a real comfort level.

The interesting part about this first phase is that neither displays much of the side of their personalities or lives that might be unflattering. It's all about making a positive presentation. So, really, you get less than a full view of the person because you're both putting your best self forward.

Everyone does it and it's not necessarily wrong. It just extends the first stage of a relationship. When you know really know that person—some of the flaws and all—you know you have moved on to the next phase.

And that next phase, enduring conflict, usually involves disagreements or conflict about one thing or another. Why? Because you have relaxed and let down your guard and allowed your true self to shine through. Fighting is a part of it. Fighting fair will get you beyond the disagreements.

There was a guy who got close to the woman he was dating. He shared that he was having a difficult time with the mother of his child. She was bitter about the breakup and berated him with deep-penetrating insults that pushed him to the brink. Of course, because they had a young child together, they had to continue to deal with each other, even as the man was growing a new relationship.

Well, once that new relationship ended, the ex-girlfriend got dirty. She told him, "I guess your baby's momma was right about you."

Ouch. That was totally unfair—and just plain old mean. It's called not fighting fair.

In the movie *Malice*, Alec Baldwin is a doctor under investigation for improper practices. During a deposition, instead of ranting and raving about the process that he considers insulting, Baldwin delivers a calm but pointed monologue that gets his point across. He never raises his voice. But he makes his points effectively.

That approach—to not raise your voice or be combative—could be the saving grace in inevitable arguments about finances, trust, how often you have sex, whatever the issues will be. And there will be issues. That is unavoidable with two people coming together. It is all about how you handle them.

Happy couples fight and argue but with respect. Unhappy couples argue like *The War of the Roses*. And that is not pretty.

One way to offset inevitable arguments is to make agreements at the outset of the relationship. Example: Agree that you will not make personal attacks when you are mad. Agree that you will not go to bed before hashing out all differences. Agree that you will not scream at each other. Agree that you will end all disagreements with a hug.

You can come up with others. The point is, create some parameters that will help you navigate through the tough spots that are bound to happen. Of course, you have to stick to the agreements once you commit to them.

It is the same way as the last stage of a relationship: making a commitment. You build something with someone that you believe is special, or at least has the potential to be special. Being committed to it will not only sustain it, but it will take it to the next level.

When people hear commitment they immediately go to cheating, which is fair. That's a serious, deal-breaking act. When you agree to marriage or a monogamous relationship, you must not stray. You want to tear down a relationship? Cheat. It will do it every time. And nine times out of ten, you will regret taking such a leap. It usually is some temporary gratification that is not worth the trouble it costs.

Still, being committed is about much more than going outside of the relationship. It's as much as how you function *inside* the relationship. Meaning, when your mate disappoints you, are you committed enough to work through that issue?

If he loses his job and, consequentially has financial issues, will you stay committed to supporting him? If he has health issues, will you stay committed or will you abandon him because it is too much of a burden to be his caretaker or help him recover?

Those kinds of concerns are raised frequently, and it is up to you, as a partner in the relationship, to handle them with skill and grace. If you truly care about and love your mate, your commitment will not waver in the fact of drama. It will get stronger—and it will hold you together.

THE NEED TO BE NEEDED: What I have seen in my relationships, in myself and virtually everyone I know, is that most of us need to feel like we are needed. It's a human condition that almost all of us share. That's one of the reasons we all desire someone special in our lives—to fill that void. And there should be no shame in needing the emotional connection you develop with someone.

For a man, it is most difficult because men are generally uncomfortable feeling vulnerable. Telling someone they need them is tantamount to telling her you can hurt me, which is a very uncomfortable place for a man. But if the man is able to trust his woman, he will be expressive and his actions will show his emotional ties to her.

When we have that emotional connection, we set ourselves up for a really meaningful relationship. There is a genuine caring and commitment that comes with it—when handled properly.

That is something to be treasured, not manipulated. Many times, though, when people realize that you need them, they use that to their advantage. They become arrogant and less attentive. They believe they can get away with more because you need them. I bring that up because you have to identify when that rises in your partner and be able to address it with calm to help it to stop.

I also bring it up because you could find yourself in that position, where you know a man needs you or is relying on you and you use that to an advantage. It is not good either way. You might not consciously try to manipulate him, but it takes a smart, keen person to realize that he/she is changing and manipulating a situation.

Having someone need you is an honor, a coveted position because you have an emotional connection. That gives you every chance for a beautiful relationship. It is to be honored, not manipulated.

KEITH'S KEY: One of the things most men have learned is that women have a biological clock that seems to tick faster than normal time. That has to be the reason they size up a man and have him in a serious relationship with her after the first date. Sure, there are men who have told women, "You're gonna be my wife," shortly after meeting them. But in many more cases, it is women who are looking to blow a first meeting into a future husband. That only puts you in a position of forcing the issue. It's like this: If you put it out there that you really *want* a man, you will find yourself ignoring issues with him that you ordinarily would not let pass. But your mindset is so intent on fulfilling your ambition that you will lower your standards to make it a reality. Instead, understand there are relationship steps or phases that have to be completed before you should declare him as the love of your life.

Additionally, understand that when you do get involved, get involved. Be a part of that man's life. Understand who he is, his likes and dislikes and cater to those areas. That's how you become connected to someone. Do all that without ignoring your own needs, which you should readily express to your mate.

CHAPTER TWENTY-ONE
FAMILY MATTERS MATTER

So, there was this man, an only child, his mother's source of pride and achievement. He was thirty-eight years old, with a wife and two children. He was a professional, a director of a corporation with dozens of employees in his charge. And yet, he was still "Mommy's baby." That was a problem.

It did not have to be a problem, but because his mother believed it was her place to control the son, it became a real touchy issue within his family. Worse, the son found it acceptable that he let his mom control his life and family.

If you think Loretta Devine's character in the movie *Jumping the Broom* was an exaggeration, well, think again. There are countless extreme cases of the mother ruling her grown son to the point where it interferes with the relationship of her son and his wife.

Take, for example, the case of the guy I mentioned. We'll call him Weakling. Weakling's mother divorced her husband a decade before her son married. She never remarried—never even dated another man. She wrapped her entire world around her son's, manipulating him at every turn for everything: money, time, attention, labor…whatever came to her mind. Whether it was done intentionally to cause conflict in his life did not matter. The wife grew to be distraught at how her husband allowed his mom to control her life.

It got to the point where he would abandon his responsibilities at home in order to please his mother. Because the wife did not know how to deal with his actions, she made matters worse by degrading him.

"Momma's Boy," she called him.

"Punk…"

"Soft..."

She figured that challenging his manhood would make him step up and behave the way she believed he should. All it did was make him more defensive and more combative—and more determined to do exactly what she didn't want him to do.

Many men are lucky. Their mother-in-laws are non-intrusive and do not seek to rule their lives.

But, as with Weakling, this is a serious problem that cannot be overstated. And it's a problem that lingers and seldom gets better because most people just do not know how to manage that situation. But here are some ways for you and your mate to avoid falling victim to in-law interference.

POSITIVE OVER NEGATIVE. As much as it may pain you, search high and low to be upbeat about your in-laws' existence in your life. Point out the benefits of their roles. It could be that they are outstanding baby-sitters of your kids, allowing you and your husband a chance to get away from the grind of work and home life. It could be that they have chipped in financially when you all were starting out and trying to get on solid footing. It could be that the mother provided family recipes that your children loved. They provide joy to your children's lives with their attention and stories, and the kids love being spoiled by them.

Whatever it is, look at the benefits of their existence in your lives instead of the negatives. You'll find that being positive about it will help you to prevent burying yourself in frustration.

And you can look at it this way: Your husband is an offspring of your in-laws, so they cannot be all bad. Think about other cases where the in-laws are overwhelming. You know, the it-could-always-be-worse position. Make sure the glass is half-full and not half-empty when it comes to looking at the in-laws in your life.

NO IN-FIGHTING WITH IN-LAWS. Even if the in-laws overstep their boundaries, deal with them with respect and calm. Every little thing is not worth you commenting or creating a stir. In fact, it would be wiser to ignore or dismiss any negativity that comes from them. Many times, on political, religion, or family issues, there could be vast disagreements in the positions.

The best move if that should happen: agree to disagree. After all, they are your elders. And what harm does it do to show deference? None. It actually shows respect, which they can only appreciate.

You might see areas of weakness in their thoughts, actions, personalities. But if it does not bring down the family, it is better to avoid an argument that would promote them having harsh feelings about you.

DO NOT TAKE THEIR POSITIONS PERSONALLY. Unless your in-laws are particularly hip, you can bet that they will be critical of, for example, what you allow your kids to wear, how late you allow them to stay out, what you allow them to watch on television, or even say to their parents.

"In my day, kids knew their place," your mother-in-law might say to you. "Kids did what they were told. You let this child get away with too much."

If you take that personally, you're subject to get really ugly because you want to raise your child the way you want to raise your child—without others' input. But to avoid a big blow-up, you have to understand that she was only offering her opinion, which everyone is entitled to have. It was not an attack on you.

When you take it as that, you can take a deep breath and move on without so much anxiety burning within. And, more importantly, you will avoid a dispute.

The other part of this is that you have to be confident in the way you are raising your kids, treating your husband, and running your home. It might not make you feel great that your mother-in-law does not agree with your methods. But if you know you are doing your best and believe in your methods, it is okay that she thinks it should be done a different way.

There is more than one way to achieve most missions. And you know your children better than anyone else, so that should bring you comfort—and not turmoil.

KILL THEM WITH KINDNESS. Whether you have enough friends or not, you can at least try to take away some of that edge the in-laws might have toward you by being as cordial and friendly as possible. I don't mean kissing up to them, but I do mean engaging them with conversation—about the kids, their child, their lives, what's going on in the world.

Conversation is the best way to learn about someone. And so, the more you are able to show your smarts and consciousness, and that you like them, it gives them more insight into who you are. Plus, the more you see and talk to them, the more you will understand them, which can only help give you insight and perspective that will aid you in knowing how to deal with them.

It also will help to invite them to your home just because, and not strictly on holidays or birthdays. It will make them feel wanted and liked by you, which should help them in their comfort level and confidence in you.

PSYCHE YOURSELF OUT. Ever seen an athletic team prepare for a game? Just before they run on the court or the field, they jump up and down and knock each other around in an effort to get pumped up about the game they are about to play. Those pre-game antics help put them in a mood to go out and perform their best.

Well, you can take a similar approach to managing your in-laws. I'm not saying you should jump around. But you should put yourself in a place of peace and a place of feeling good and lively. If you let that attitude carry over, hopefully you will be able to deal with whatever comes your way in an upbeat fashion. When you're feeling good, you don't want to let someone bring you down, and so your efforts to stay emotionally uplifted are increased over going into it, dreading what *could* happen.

Having a less-that-pleasant attitude about seeing them only makes you more susceptible to having a meltdown should there be a disagreement or something said or done that you do not like.

As counter-intuitive as it may sound, *feelings follow actions.* Before an encounter with your in-laws, take the time to put yourself in a friendly, calm frame of mind, or at least try to act that way when you see them. If you go into any situation acting angry, defensive, or suspicious, you'll invoke that emotion in yourself, and likely a negative reaction from others. If you're feeling more light-hearted, you won't be as quick to take offense.

IN-LAWS HAVE RIGHTS, TOO. Traditionally, the grandparents take on a role with their grandkids that is totally opposite of the way they were with their children. If they were disciplinarians with their sons and daughters, you can bet they will be far less stern with the grandchildren.

Where their children were not allowed to eat sweets at random, they tend to lay the candy, cookies and cake on their grandkids, which, many times, could be contrary to what you'd like them to eat. It may be hard to accept, but that's one of the traditional privileges grandparents have always had, and so you have to adjust your thinking around that if it conflicts with your thoughts.

How many times did you run to your grandmother or grandfather when your parents denied you something you wanted? Your mother and father probably were seething, but they also probably let it go because they knew it made the grandparents feel good.

No harm was done and the grandparents felt great. That's a win-win situation. And that's what it comes down to—is this a battle worth fighting and ruining an important relationship? Of course, if we're talking about something that truly compromises your hard-core beliefs and values, then that is another story. But letting the kids eat junk food or stay up a little later with the grandparents causes little pain. Above all, it should make you feel good to make your in-laws feel good.

Now, back to Weakling. This is among the more serious issues you can have with a mother-in-law because her efforts are really impacting your household and relationship with your husband. How do you deal with it?

Well, for one, have a heart-to-heart with your husband. Let him know you admire his commitment to his mom and that you would never look to come between their relationship. But remind him that he has a family that should come first, and that his responsibility is to prevent a negative effect on his home life.

You would be able to see how being pulled in two directions at once would impact him, in his physical health or mental stress. Let him know it would not be disrespecting his mother to let her know his family comes first. Let him know that you love him, but ignoring his family for his mother, spending money intended for the home on his mother, and generally siding with his mother on most issues threatens his marriage. Let him know you have been patient and understanding but your endurance and tolerance are over.

If this does not put a charge in him, then it likely is time to make the phone call to his mother. Of course, that is a delicate call to make. You do not want to put her in a defensive position and you do not want to be disrespectful to her, either. So, it would be wise to let her know that you are concerned about your husband because he's dividing himself—and his finances—between her and his family. Let her know that you have seen physical changes or detected mental or emotional stress because of this.

Doing it this way puts the in-law in a position of feeling like she should be a part of the solution more so than the problem. This is all psychological. Perhaps the in-law will examine her role and decide the best thing she could do would be to work in unison with you to turn around the son's actions.

All of this is a waste if you have a mother-in-law from hell, someone who just does not like you or *anyone* her son dates, no matter how hard you try to make it work. In these sad and tough cases, it is up to the husband to get a grip and find a balance. Rest assured you're going to have to help him get there.

But the family dynamics do not start and end with in-laws. I know friends whose marriages or relationships are impaired because of their relationships with their brothers and sisters—and even cousins.

There are brothers who want to move into your home until they "get themselves together." But they do not want to pay any rent or a utility bill or groceries. There are sisters who are jealous that you have a family and take every opportunity they can to undermine your relationship with your husband. And there are cousins who believe they have every right to judge you and your spouse on everything you do. And these are just some of the mild examples of how family can come barging into your lives like a boulder.

It is hard to turn your back on a loved one. You actually should take pride in helping them in any way you can. But there could come a point where your kindness is being disrespected. And that's where the trouble comes in.

Your husband has had it with the drama; you find it difficult to not be there for family. Or vice versa. Somewhere, somehow, some way, you have to come together to get peace in your house.

Never would I say kick family to the curb—well, only if they deserve to be kicked to the curb. I'm for family as much as the next person. But let's be real: Family can be more of a headache than anyone else.

CHAPTER TWENTY-TWO

GETTING MARRIED? GET READY!!!

You are about to tie, or you are thinking about tying, the knot. Good for you. Marriage is the ultimate relationship. It can be a beautiful thing when the right two people connect at the right time for the right reasons and do the right things. But there is a lot to it, a lot to prepare for before jumping the broom.

I'm not the most religious guy in the world. But I go to church and I know God has blessed me many times over. I say that to say this: The men and women of the cloth understand the spiritual and moral significance of marriage, and so I would suggest receiving premarital counseling before saying "I do."

Having a third-party, an impartial person from your church who understands the dynamics of marriage, provides the kind of foundation going into the wedding that will strengthen you and your fiancé. And when the two of you are on one accord, you band together in order to form a strong, almost unbeatable team.

Your religion is your religion—and there are those who are atheists—so I will not get into one denomination over the other. But there is something spiritual about the connecting of two people in a relationship, an understanding that certainly can provide a measure of perspective that could help in the trying times of marriage that are bound to come.

And that really is not about religion. It's about a state of being. If you're spiritually grounded in who you are to your mate, and what your marriage is to you, you have a much better chance of not only surviving the inevitable drama, but thriving over the course of the relationship.

Of course, that cannot be the only foundation of a successful marriage/

relationship. There are many other factors to master BEFORE you get married that bear your attention. There are clearly a lot of other things to consider. Issues will arise, no matter how thorough you plot and plan. That's just how it is. But you need order in your life and everything you do. If you plan to move from one city to the next, you don't just do it. You find the right neighborhood for your family in the area with the best schools, you look at the benefits of the city, the cost of living, the housing market, etc. So you certainly should not go into a marriage without a comprehensive game plan on how to make it work—or to at least minimize potential drama. Here are some considerations:

WORD OF MOUTH. Whoever heard of someone admitting to his/her fiancé that they have the potential to cheat during the marriage? Even if you promise you won't get mad and plead for honest communication, it would be silly for someone to admit something so horrible. But the point is that you have to ask the question, meaning you must encourage open, free-flowing communication all the time about everything. That has to be established before the wedding. And when I say everything, I mean *everything*. You're about to become one, live in the same space, call each other husband and wife…you should be able to discuss anything with that person if no one else. And the way to push that is to have constant dialogue about your life, your desires, your concerns. This has to be established before marriage because many people are hesitant about sharing all their thoughts or feelings, thinking it would be nagging. Well, that's all about how your concerns are delivered. If you're whining and complaining, then, yes, your mate likely will grow tired of your mouth. But if you bring your issues to the table in a rational, conversational manner, you will get the results you want, which should be a thoughtful, controlled conversation. If anger or frustration laces your expression, you will find yourself getting increasingly angry and not getting the point across that you wish to address. At the same time, those concerns will be coming your way. You have to talk before marriage about being able to hear what your mate says to you. If you practice hearing or absorbing concerns, you will minimize the angst that can come with marriage.

BEND SO YOU DON'T BREAK. Your way cannot be the only way. Period. Selfishness has to go out of the window or down the toilet. A marriage is a bond, and no matter how you grew up or what you experienced prior to walking down that aisle, you must go into the marriage with a spirit of compromise. Simply put, you cannot get your way all the time. For some people, men and women, that's a hard ideal to swallow. But if you order your life to please your mate, then the idea of accepting someone else's opinion and having honest negotiations about decisions will make for a much better living situation. And this is not something that is to be done for a portion of the marriage. This compromising nature must exist throughout the marriage, on both sides.

Let's say that in your single life, you and your girlfriends spent each Saturday afternoon going to the mall. As a married woman, that activity should not totally stop because you must still maintain some of your individuality. However, you should be open to the idea of forgoing the shopping to accommodate your man if he has plans for you. It's the same way if he played golf most weekends with his boys. If you have something significant planned, he should be willing to pass on golf on occasion to join you in another activity. Even though those were your lifestyles before marriage, after marriage you have to bend on some of those "traditions." But it must be discussed and agreed to before the vows are taken. This is important, though: You should not ask your new husband (and he shouldn't ask you) to give up all his independent social events. You do that and you can bet there will be serious resentment, which will foster an ugly situation. Conversely, the willingness to compromise will make your mate feel good about you—and also make him more likely to equally compromise. And so, together, you are helping to keep your home a happy place.

YOU GOTTA PAY TO PLAY: Finances can be the root of upheaval in a marriage. Who makes it? Who spends it? Who manages it? This has to be discussed at length, openly and honestly, as part of your premarital preparations. What do you want to purchase together? How will you achieve it? Working hard together to make sure credit scores are elevated is important. A lot of thought and strategy must go into the finances part because studies indicate that, after infidelity, money problems are next in reasons why couples divorce. You have to figure where the paychecks will go—ideally, there should be a shared account and at least an individual savings. Are there student loans to be tackled? You have to develop the strategy on building together, but someone has to handle the day-to-day paying of the bills. Who will do that? This element of premarital arrangements is vital to your survival. There are many books and classes you could take together on managing finances, building your credit score and saving money. Take advantage of those to give yourselves an advantage going into the marriage. Lastly on finances, you should probably develop a five-year plan on where you'd like to live, how much travel you'd like to have done, how much money you'd like to have in your savings. Giving yourself a goal always works best because you have something to shoot for.

HOUSEHOLD CHORES. The days of the woman doing all the housework have long passed. And, frankly, it's just not fair that the woman be responsible for the entire upkeep of the home. Well, let me backtrack. If she wants to take on that responsibility by herself, then it's all good. But if she believes it should be a shared responsibility, then that discussion is vital before getting hitched. Why is it vital? Because if the man believes the woman must cook the dinner, serve him and then wash the dishes after eating…and she does not agree with that, you're looking at real problems. Resentment. Anger. Frustration. Animosity. So, the safest and smartest route is to set up some household guidelines. Chores that require physical exertion like taking out the trash or mowing the lawn are usually considered a man's job, and I agree with that. But he should also be willing to wash the dishes if you went out and shopped for the groceries, cooked the meal and served it to him. Right? It really comes down to fairness. It is only fair that I cook for my woman on occasion and wash the dishes if she cooks. That kind of agreement actually eliminates any potential for upheaval. And it promotes working together. It's the same with other household duties: cleaning bathrooms, vacuuming, raking leaves. The idea is that figuring it out before you become a married couple works better than doing it on the fly.

HOLIDAY JEER: One of the biggest battles young couples end up having to go through is where to spend the major holidays. If you are from different cities and traditionally spend Thanksgiving or Christmas with your family and your future husband with his, how do you figure out where to go once married? That's something that has to be worked through, right? Maybe you go to his family's home for Thanksgiving and yours for Christmas. Or vice versa. Going in separate directions is not the best option. When you have children, it is very likely you'd like to develop your own tradition of hosting Thanksgiving and/or Christmas at your home. Whatever you decide, you must decide it together, rationally, and in advance, to prevent conflict that comes with a disagreement as personal as family.

TIME OUT? If you plan to have kids or already have children, then how you discipline them could very well be a concern. If you were raised by parents that enforced "time out"—a period of time alone in a corner or room—when you got into trouble, that might conflict big time with your soon-to-be husband who was whipped with a belt when he got into mischief as a child. It stands to reason that we discipline our children the way we were disciplined. But it is really important to come to terms with the methods before it is time to make an emotional decision. I can see it now: you believing the child should be punished and the father believing he needs a whipping. The child standing there between you two, his head going back and forth as he watches you argue over what will happen to him. Not a good look. With children, there has to be a united front at all times, a show of authority and force so they know they cannot move from one parent to the next after being rebuffed. If nothing else, if there is a disagreement on how to deal with a discipline issue, the conversation to come to an agreement should take place away from the child. There should not be an argument in front of the child about how the child will be disciplined.

AND THE BIBLE SAYS. In the South, most everyone goes to church. Not everyone, but a very high percentage attend on Sundays because it is part of the culture in that region of the country. If you and your fiancé do not establish a church routine, then there is the possibility of true drama because family, politics and religion are the three hot-button topics that bring out all kinds of emotions. If church is an important part of your life, it would help you to see if your future mate has a similar interest. Worshipping together, as a family, is important. It happens a lot that the wife ends up going to church alone because the husband just does not want to go. Other issues around church could be present: What if he's a Baptist and you're a Catholic? What if he believes in tithing and you don't? All those questions need to be answered and resolved *before* marriage.

On a larger scale, planning years in advance is a good idea. It at least gives you a framework, an outline from which to work. Things happen—you can count on that—that could alter the plan. But before slipping that ring on his finger at the altar, it is best to look forward with some shared idea of where you want to go.

THE FIRST YEAR: In those first 365 days, you should have established a rhythm to married life. You should know each other even better than before and, therefore, be closer than you ever had been. All the basic questions should have been addressed and acted on, like where you will live, what is the family budget, etc. The honeymoon should last about that entire year. You should have made romance a serious part of your life. This is the portion of marriage where you look at your ring every day in amazement and you're excited when someone calls you Mrs. Jones, or when you hear your man say, "This is my wife," or someone asks you, "How's your husband?" Anything that indicates you're married makes you smile and feel great inside about life. You're smiling after a year because you have gotten over the initial awkwardness of merging households and establishing that rhythm and you're at a place where you can look forward to the future.

IN THE THIRD YEAR: By the end of the third year, you are veterans of the marriage game. You should know each other through and through, which allows for you to thoroughly plan ahead for the next several years of your married life. A child could be a part of the mix by now—or you could be planning for a kid—giving your marriage more depth. But with a child comes more planning: Is your home large enough? How do you set up daycare? Who will get up at night when the child cries? Finances become even more critical. A budget has to be established that will include the child and his/her care, food, clothes, insurance, doctor's visits, etc. An agreement has to be made on cutting back on spending before the baby comes. If a child was already a part of the equation, he/she is three years older, and there are more costs associated with a kid getting older because they are involved in more activities. If children are not in the plan, then you should have been working toward building a nice nest egg for home improvements, car upgrades, a new house…whatever way you'd like to go as a couple.

THE SIX-YEAR ITCH: You know about the infamous "seven-year itch." It is around that time that marriages can get monotonous and predictable. That's why I say reevaluate at six years to get ahead of the curve. Be proactive. Make an honest and thorough assessment of what has taken place in the union, how well you have followed the goals established and break down where improvements need to be made. Is the communication where you'd like it to be—open and honest and respectful? Are you supporting each other on career goals? Has the sex life been consistent and satisfying? Have you made choices together on the kids' schools and looked into future schools. Plans are just that, plans. Nothing is unchangeable. When you look ahead to six years of marriage, it should be with the idea that you've established a rock-solid foundation. So if the plans need to be changed, you are comfortable enough and trust each other enough to make alterations together smoothly and almost effortlessly.

A DECADE IN: There is never a comfort period in a relationship, but you should be proud to make it to ten years. That says a lot has been right about your planning and you have fulfilled some of the goals you set together. Even if your plans were not carried out as expected, you made adjustments that worked and your family can still be intact if you, prior to marriage, made commitments on communication, compromising, working together and devotion to each other. You would have determined more about children— and probably have had all you're going to by that point. But what schools would they attend? Public or private? A college education fund? Family vacations? Again, nothing is etched in stone. But to have had in-depth conversations about where you hoped to be surely will give you a guide to where you will end up.

KEITH'S KEY: It's like this: What you do *before* you get married is just as important as what you do *in* your marriage. It is then when you talk and talk and talk about the future, your plans, how you will handle many aspects of your lives together. That's when you build the foundation. It's much better to do that than to get into it and try to do it by the seat of your pants. All that does is increase the chances for disagreements, which increase the chances for being annoyed, frustrated, disappointed and resentful. None of those emotions are positive, meaning you bring into play toxic vibes early on in your relationship. So, talk to each other to get some common ground and shared goals. And those goals should be short-term and long-term. Best and most important of all, they should be done together. To map out how you want to live your lives together will give you heightened confidence that you are with the right person and that you will be able to have a marriage that is fun, lively, exciting and fulfilling. And when you think about it, that's the way it should be.

CHAPTER TWENTY-THREE
HOW TO *NOT* MESS UP A RELATIONSHIP

Making a relationship last forever is not easy. But don't get scared. It's not impossible, either. A lot of times, though, it's not about making it work; it's about not messing it up.

We all have an ability to get in our own way with ideas and attitudes about relationships that are not only wrong, but also work counter to your goals. In other words, you hurt yourself by overdoing it.

You've probably been a part of relationships that flamed out like a shooting star or dragged out like mud sliding down a hillside. In either case, it is often about what we do to mess things up rather than what someone does—or does not do—to us. So, it is a mentality involved that can help you steady the course of the relationship instead of tilting it over.

TIT FOR TAT: He did this so you do that. You showed him, right? No, actually, you didn't. What you showed was your competitive side, which is what a relationship should not be about—not a healthy relationship, anyway. Tit-for-tat is silly and childish and a relationship killer. A relationship is not a game that you compete in to win or that you are looking to get even on. You shouldn't be consumed with winning a battle of what you do or how something goes or anything that requires you to decide together on an issue. People's competitive genes or paranoia often make them feel like they have to get the upper hand in various situations around their mates. The idea should be to soothe each other—not cut each other's throats to get what you want. When you're in competitive relationships, you're always seeking the edge or advantage so you can hold it over your mate, as if it makes you better or stronger to diminish someone you are supposed to care about in a special way. One of the common and most-used competitive tactics is when you tell your partner something and he/she comes back later and tries to use it against you. That is totally wrong and unfair and it's the best way to create a huge argument. It also could make your mate shut down on sharing with you because you tried to use it as a point in an argument instead of the spirit in which it was told to you. In short, don't do it.

HERE'S THAT WORD AGAIN...TRUST: I talk about trust every day—on my radio show or in my own life—because it is that important to a successful relationship. Not having trust, or being untrustworthy, is a detriment to a relationship that I cannot even put into words. We have all been there, where we just did not believe in the person we were with, but we *wanted* to believe. But the lack of trust was eating us up inside, making us doubt every word out of their mouths. You can, and will, mess up a relationship if you carry your lack of trust from a previous relationship into your current situation. No one wants to be hounded by, or even be with, someone who does not trust him. And you do not want that in reverse. If you're going to be with someone, the trust has to be built and sustained. Hammering some-one—or being hammered—messes with the strength of the relationship and will tear it down.

I remember a case where a woman I was dating asked if it was okay for her to go to lunch with a guy she knew. If my trust level with her was not solid, I would have said, "Hell, no." And she might have been offended because I didn't show that I believed in her. But I did trust her and she had the lunch and that was that. I hear all the time, "I trust you, but I don't trust those women out there." That comment can go both ways. But the reality is that it is not about the other person. It's always about you. So I knew the guy the woman went to lunch with didn't just go because he was hungry. He was trying to get with her. But he cannot make any noise if she doesn't allow him. It doesn't matter if others are interested in you. It's about what you do to build trust so that your man believes you'll be true to him. Now, there are other women I have dated where I would not have been so comfortable saying, "yes." I knew who they were based on what they showed me...There's also the trust issue of feeling confident enough to share your intimate feelings with your mate and knowing he will not judge you by them. That can be just as devastating. You see, we start to get all high and mighty when someone reveals something that we do not understand or would not do. But that's not the way to be. We have to accept what was said and appreciate that the person cared enough to be honest with us and not be judgmental or hold their thoughts against them.

SHUTTING UP TO SHUT DOWN: Ever been with someone who, out of the blue, starts complaining about something you said or did a month prior? And you're like, "What are you talking about?"

That's the result of something bothering him but, instead of bringing it up to discuss, he held it in and let it fester and build up to something significant in his mind. And you're totally thrown off because you might not even recall exactly the incident or words he brings up. This is a problem.

Way too many couples suppress stuff that should be addressed when the problem arises. But why do they hold back? Well, a few reasons, I believe. One, women, in particular, do not want to seem like a pest or a nag, someone who drives a man crazy with an issue about every little thing. So they hold it in until they are about to burst—and it usually comes out harsher than intended, starting a knock-down, drag-out.

Then there is the case of those who hold back because they do not want to hurt their mate's feelings. That's a nice gesture, but the reality is that it is unhealthy to shut down when there is an issue—unhealthy for you and for the relationship. Almost every issue that you consider important should be a point of discussion. It is all in *how* you discuss your concerns.

Attacking someone about an issue never gets the results you want. It might feel good to get it off your chest, but it only pushes someone in a corner, a corner they will be willing to fight out of to make their points. So, be delicate but firm. Understand your mate. If you do understand him, you know his pressure points. Avoid them. After all, the idea is to make your point and solve an issue, right?

SAY WHAT? If your man is talking to you—I don't care how tired you are or how distracted you might be—listen. It might seem like gibberish to you; you have your own things on your mind. But that's part of the role of being together: You are each other's sounding boards.

And in difficult times, when you might not want to hear what he has to say because it is critical of you...listen. If you really listen, you will learn how he thinks and how to avoid a similar issue in the future. And "really listening" means hearing and digesting what he says, not nodding your head and preparing your comeback. I have been in arguments with women who are so eager to defend themselves they don't even hear exactly what I'm saying. So, they end up arguing about something that I did not even say or think.

Above all, giving your mate your full attention is giving him respect. And of course, all of this goes both ways. You should not accept your mate not listening to you. But your behavior toward him can dictate how he responds to you. Remember that.

MO MONEY, MO MONEY. When you are single and especially a woman (not stereotyping, just giving it to you real), the mall is your best and closest friend. At the very least, you have a date with it several times a month, and just about every weekend. But that's okay...when you're single. Then, you can shop till you drop, get up, shop again and drop again. It's no one's business but yours. But as a married woman, those random, spur-of-the-moment shopping binges have to be reined in some. As much as it might bother you to hold back, you have to consider the household, your man, the children (if you have any) and the bills. For independent people, that can be quite an adjustment. You are asked to, at once, be mindful of your spending in a way that you had not even truly considered before. (Never mind that shopping sprees were likely not the thing to do anyway. You had to handle the financial burden of that.) To ask you to discuss spending your money certainly can be an adjustment. But it is a part of being in a married or co-habitation arrangement. It seems more people want to keep their money separate from their spouses, making for drama if one side does not agree. Please do not spend money as if it is your money and yours alone—no matter what your past may have been. Respect the family structure. If you both decide on separate accounts, that's fine, too—as long as you do not spend frivolously and have the funds when needed for household and family responsibilities. Sometimes men go overboard with spending, too, and so part of your responsibility as the woman is to make him see his responsibility as a man in the relationship. If either of you are not willing to bend on the spending, that is not good for the future.

CLOSER THAN CLOSE. The gap between loving your mate and being dependent on him is paper-thin. Loving is good. Dependency…not so much. You should not have the burden of being someone's whole world. It's awesome to be loved and to be the center of someone's world. That's comforting. But it is truly a burden to have someone rely on you for his happiness. It's hard enough being happy in the world. It's quite difficult—and unfair—to be responsible for another adult's cheer. How do you know someone is too dependent on you or you on someone? When you hear, "I cannot live without you." Or you say that.

We've all been head-over-heels in love before and believe, at that time, the world stops and starts to that person's command. But it's not healthy—and you're setting yourself up for major disappointment to put that much weight on someone.

Additionally, you should not be a financial crutch to anyone. Everyone should carry his/her own weight. If you rely on someone to carry you financially, you will stick around just for that purpose. And vice versa. And who wants that?

REMOTE CONTROL. It is one thing to care about someone's well-being. But it's another thing to try to control their eating habits. It's one thing to suggest what someone wears; it's another to purchase all their clothes. Those are examples of a controlling person, someone who wants things their way or no way. They really can mess up a relationship.

Don't be that girl. It's not cute. You truly could have your mate's best interests at heart. But that does not mean it's acceptable to determine how he acts, where he goes, what he wears, what he eats…etc.

I know a guy whose woman was very health-conscious. She ate the right foods and worked out and wanted her man to do the same. So, whenever he ordered out at dinner, she would demand that he change his order to meet her satisfaction. To keep the peace, he would give in and order what she wanted. But he was not happy.

As mates, the most we can do is make suggestions—some more strongly than others, depending on the situation. But we have to let it go after that. Trying to control how and what someone eats is simply too much. It borders on selfishness that you believe your way is the only way. Grown people are like kids in some cases: You try to force them to do something and they will do the opposite. And a woman controlling her man hardly makes him seem manly. A woman controlled by a man is hardly womanly.

BYGONES BE GONE. If you are in a relationship with Jimmy, be in that relationship with Jimmy. The back-sliding to old boyfriends has to stop. If you liked him so much, you should be with him. And the same goes for men. The last thing I want to hear from someone I'm dating is that she's talking to her "ex" or planning to have lunch with her old boyfriend. Really? Seriously?

I understand what that's all about. I have women I dated who call me occasionally, saying they're just saying hello or trying to catch up. That might be the case, too. But if the woman I'm seeing gets wind of it, she has every right to be concerned because of the history of back-sliding in relationships.

There is a familiarity with your "ex" that makes going too far easy. He knows you so well that he knows what to say, when to say it and how to say it. He knows your weak spots, your turn-ons. And because you have shared so much, he believes he has license to say that which he would not say to someone else. Surely, if your man was communicating regularly—an infrequent text or phone call to say hello is harmless—with his old woman, you would not be comfortable. You'd be very uncomfortable, in fact.

Bottom line: He's gone, so be gone. Even if the ex's intentions are genuine, it serves no good purpose to see him or be a fixture in his life. You broke up for a reason. Remember that.

KEITH'S KEY: A relationship is yours to own, not mess up. So be conscious of your actions. Let things happen organically, naturally. Forcing the issue or controlling the issue only puts your man on the defense—and that's not a good place to be. Be a good listener and a participant in the relationship. Shutting down when you are upset never helps. Speaking in rational tones works. And, again, trust that you are with the right person. That will allow you to relax in the relationship—and enjoy it.

CHAPTER TWENTY-FOUR

BLACK LOVE

The numbers say black love is down and divorces are up. I say give me a break. We love as much now as we ever have. I know because I listen to callers five nights a week for hours talking about it, seeking ways to make it flourish.

I think that if we keep in mind what true love should represent, we will be more committed to locating it, nurturing it and sustaining it. For me, black love is about family and children and love.

Family means a lot. It is a group of people with the same bloodlines that love, honor and protect each other and grow together. It is a beautiful thing, a family led by two loving parents. It is the prime opportunity to show children what true love and affection are about. If kids see it growing up in their household with their parents, don't you think they are more likely to grow into what they witnessed?

That alone is another inspiration for writing this book. There is power in strong relationships that are powered by love. The statistics are what they are. But I contend that we love, and no study can make me believe that we are less in love, or passionate, or passionate about being in love.

Yes, we see more families led by single women. But these women represent strength and dedication, especially to their children. I talk to these women all the time; they want the best for their kids. And if a man is not around to support them, these women show their kids what strength and commitment are all about. That's much better than having a man around who offers less than what they need.

In March 2012, there was the 8th Annual National Black Marriage Day, organized by the Wedded Bliss Foundation. The intent was to promote healthy relationships in black communities and the benefits of two-parent families for children. Around the country, many married couples renewed their vows, with some couples even marrying on that day. In Milwaukee, more than three hundred couples renewed their vows that day.

And there were countless other celebrations of National Black Marriage Day around the country. That this was even created speaks to the concern of the organizers of the black family structure, which is legitimate.

To my way of thinking, we can help establish love in our lives by keeping in mind that our children are watching and we should always be about setting examples for them.

Even as a single mom—and you all are among the strongest creatures on earth—you have to be more diligent than anyone about your love life around your children. How? First of all, a man who is interested in you should not even meet your child for several months. I know of so many women who have flaunted their children in front of some guy they just met because he was cute or because they had no one to watch their child at the time he was to be around. That's no excuse.

Again, kids absorb everything, and if you introduce them to "Joe" this month, who is to say he will be around next month? Then you meet "Pete" the following month and put him in front of your kids, too. Six weeks later, you decide "Pete" was not up to your standards and he's gone. But along comes "Mike." Now you have your children saying hello to three different men in three months. That's not a good look.

If you think your children will not process that parade of men in your life, please think again. My point is this: Single moms, be over-the-top protective of the men you put in front of your children. They do not need to meet them. That is your relationship that you are trying to develop. Keep that separate from your kids. If you did not know, kids emulate their parents, and if you have a young daughter meeting man after man, you can bet that she believes it is acceptable to do so. It is not.

But when she comes of age, you think she's going to behave the way she has seen her mother behave or some foreign way?

And it is the same with boys. A young boy sees his mom with a series of men and he will be damaged in a few ways: 1) By nature, he is protective of his mom, and seeing these men with her impacts his already-developing instincts to protect you; and 2) He could look at women in a less-than-flattering way because of what he's seen from his mother.

It all depends on how he processes it. Overall, if we are great role models for our kids, they stand a better chance of experiencing love the way it should be experienced. They deserve the fair opportunity for nothing less.

The other way to get them there is to have real conversations with them. If you're a single mother, let your kids know that it is not the ideal situation and that they should seek true love only and that they should strive for marriage and not living together or just having kids. The goal should be about being with the right person for you in the ways that matter to you and building something significant together. That should be the goal. But it should not be the goal so much that you settle for someone you do not truly believe in with all your heart.

There has and continues to be a lot of settling for a mate because "it's time to get married" or "all my friends are married" or "I might not find someone better." Those are all terrible excuses to get married.

We have to practice and teach our kids that love and marriage are sacred, and they cannot be taken lightly. These are the words that a presiding pastor of a wedding will say to the couple:

Dearly Beloved, we are gathered together here in the sight of God—and in the face of this company—to join together this man and this woman in holy matrimony, which is commended to be honorable among all men; and therefore—is not by any—to be entered into unadvisedly or lightly—but reverently, discreetly, advisedly and solemnly. Into this holy estate these two persons present now come to be joined. If any person can show just cause why they may not be joined together—let them speak now or forever hold their peace.

Marriage is the union of husband and wife in heart, body and mind. It is intended for their mutual joy—and for the help and comfort given on another in prosperity and adversity. But more importantly—it is a means through which a stable and loving environment may be attained.

Through marriage, GROOM'S NAME and BRIDE'S NAME make a commitment together to face their disappointments—embrace their dreams—realize their hopes—and accept each other's failures. GROOM'S NAME and BRIDE'S

NAME will promise one another to aspire to these ideals throughout their lives together—through mutual understanding—openness—and sensitivity to each other.

We are here today—before God—because marriage is one of His most sacred wishes—to witness the joining in marriage of GROOM'S NAME and BRIDE'S NAME. This occasion marks the celebration of love and commitment with which this man and this woman begin their life together. And now—through me—He joins you together in one of the holiest bonds.

Wow. Does that give you a new, stronger perspective on how serious marriage is, seeing the words in writing? We've all heard them at weddings, but to see them in print and to slowly absorb them should give you a feeling of "That's what I want for myself—and my children."

New research indicates that fewer Americans are getting married than ever before. Results by the Pew Research Center in 2012 revealed that only 51 percent of adults in the United States are currently married. For African-American women, the marriage rate is even lower. And according to the Joint Center for Political and Economic Studies, by the age of thirty, nearly 81 percent of white women and 77 percent of Hispanics and Asians will marry. It also estimates that only 52 percent of black women will marry by that age.

In addition, black women are also the least likely to remarry following divorce, their study projects. Only 32 percent of black women will get married again within five years of divorce; that figure is 58 percent for white women and 44 percent for Hispanic women.

Those statistics and projections are what they are. But they do not quantify them with being HAPPY!!!!!! That should always be the primary goal. I'd like to see research on the percentage of people who are married but miserable. I know that number is way up there, so high that it likely would astonish the researchers.

That's why I said it is important to connect and/or marry only when you feel a love and connection that rocks your world. You have to go in at least believing you are with the right person, marrying for the right reasons—and not because it's the thing to do or because someone asked you or because you might not get asked again or because you always wanted to be married or because he can change or because you're tired of being single. All those "reasons" are recipes for unhappiness.

And as far as I know, we have one time on this earth. So, let's live it in a fulfilling way, with someone who loves us unconditionally. And if that some-one has to be us, then so be it. I am all for marriage—but only if you are with the person that floats your boat, and vice versa.

WAITING IT OUT

For black women hoping to overcome what seems like impossible odds—the ratio of men-to-women is lopsided—an important strategy would be to not get married early in adulthood. So many in my generation had been told as kids that their goal in life was to meet their future husband in college (or even high school) and get married at twenty-one. Some of them are still married. Many are not.

I do not know if getting married that early was a factor in their divorces, but it would not be a leap to believe being that young and married created problems that were hard to overcome.

You should get married when you believe it is the right time for you, but hopefully after giving the idea a true and thorough view. And please do not succumb to the pressure of family and friends. I am not calling out mothers, but you are good for encouraging your daughter to get married, even if you do not deep inside believe the man is ideal for her. There's something about saying "my daughter's getting married" and "my son-in-law" that gives moms a thrill. And so often, at her mother's urging, the child goes into something that she likely does feel so comfortable about to please the mom.

There is an inherent problem with being married too young—you don't know exactly who you are just yet. That makes nurturing a man and a rela-tionship at the same time pretty daunting. I'm just going to go ahead and say it: In most cases, unless you are super mature and together, people should wait until their thirties to get married.

It is then that you are established in your career, you have a firm grasp on who you are, you understand much better what a mate should look, act and feel like, and generally you are just at a better place in your life. You would be able to quantify it for some time, but I believe, anyway, that the divorce rate would drop significantly if most people got married in their thirties. That does not mean every marriage with last and prosper. But it just makes sense that both parties would be settled and able to manage all the dynamics that come with being married much better. Above all, we'd all make better, wiser decisions on whom our mates should be.

KEITH'S KEY: Believe in love and marriage, no matter what your past. But do not run to either. Let whatever is supposed to happen, happen in its own time. Having been married, I recognize that it can be a wonderful institution. But we have to make choices that fit us, not choices that look good or sound like a good idea. Choosing a mate is as important as anything you could do, and so it cannot be taken as something simple. Read again the words above that an official would recite at your wedding. If you can hold to those ideals, then you know you are marrying the right person. In the end, our kids are watching us, so set a great example on the mates you choose and choose to put around them.

CHAPTER TWENTY-FIVE
MAKE HIM RUN *TO* YOU, NOT AWAY FROM YOU

As a species, men can be as excited about women as women are about men, and yet we will remain calm about it. We do not feel the need to bombard women with attention or see them every day. At least not at the onset, anyway.

Two weeks into meeting him, you are confused as to why he returns your text messages much more slowly than before, or not at all. The phone calls become infrequent or cease altogether. You did something to spark this behavior, and many times women do not even know what it is.

In a word, it is being "clingy." You know what I mean—you like him so much that you cannot contain your glee. So, the natural thing for you is to spend more time with him, talk to him more, text him more. More, more, more. You see the potential and you want to accelerate the process. Well, relationships are not something that can be fast-forwarded. They have to be nurtured, methodically and carefully. At least that's how most men see it.

So, when there is that clash of perspectives and action, many times the man will back away without a trace—or explanation. That's wrong—weak, actually. But we know it happens more often than not. And the woman is left wondering, "What did I do wrong?"

That urge to advance the relationship—shoot, after two weeks, it's not even a relationship yet—does not comfort men. In fact, it makes men uncomfortable, like you have a plan for his life and you don't even really know him yet.

Pressing a man for time and attention works opposite your desires. Trust me, he is not impressed that you called him six times over a three-hour period, left him six voice messages and fired off a dozen text messages. That does not show how much you'd like to get with him. It shows *him* that he needs to stay away from you. That hounding is not consistent with someone a man would view as a potentially stable relationship partner.

The message you send with that kind of over-the-top expression is that you will need constant reassurances from him, that you'll be all over his Facebook page, clocking who contacts him, who he contacts, etc. Scarily, it shows that you have the potential to show up at his house unannounced, at any time.

And no man—even the most needy and insecure—wants or needs that kind of attention.

Conversely, just relax. Men enjoy the chase more than the easy conquest. There is something about a woman who knows her worth and who possesses the confidence to let the man pursue her. He will respect your calm and clear show of self-esteem. Your value to him will increase.

And here's another thing: Talking incessantly about your previous relationship does nothing to make him feel good about you. In reality, that experience has nothing to do with him, and he actually would like to discover whatever there is about you on his own.

I have had women tell me stuff like, "The last man in my life didn't know how to talk to me." Or, "he didn't like going out and having a good time. I like to enjoy myself."

All that is fine. But keep it to yourself. Telling a man what you like does not help you learn about him, which should be your goal. In learning about him you will learn about your compatibility. Think of it this way: If I don't like going to the movies, but you tell me, "I love going to the movies. My old boyfriend didn't." You think I'm going to say, "I hate the movies?" Because we're trying to get to know each other and I'm trying to make a good impression, I'm subject to say anything to get you to feel good about me. So, you spend time with this person, start to really like him and then he's comfortable enough to disappoint you with, "I really don't like going to the movies."

Yes, he should have kept it real at the beginning. But the point is to let everything flow smoothly, like a river. If he asks about your favorite pastime, tell him. But do not tell him like this: "Well, I love to go to the movies. But my last boyfriend didn't so that was a problem. All he wanted to do was sit around and watch sports. And I also had a problem with his family. They wanted to control his life. Do you know he almost missed my birthday because his mother wanted him to take her shopping? And he never cooked. I cooked all the time and he just ate and didn't even say thank you. And…"

That might be funny, but it happens. You probably have unloaded on someone like that. Put yourself in his position. How would you feel if the guy started running down his ex to you? Seems to me the wonderful thing about getting to know someone is getting to know someone. Not listening to him recite chapter and verse about how his previous relationships unfolded.

Get into the new guy's life instead of listening to his history.

There was a woman I met who was divorced. Her husband apparently had a proclivity for the ladies. In other words, he messed around on her. Beautiful, smart, fun, wonderful woman. But what made her even more appealing to me was that she never, not once, went off about how awful her ex-husband was. She did not speak of him in glowing terms, mind you. But she hardly spoke of him at all. He was the father of her son and while he disappointed her to the point where she had to leave, she chose to conceal her disdain for his actions as her husband. I always looked at her with the ultimate admiration. She could have easily called him every name in the book. Instead, she said, "I tried to make it work. I know I did everything I could. I didn't get back what I deserved and I just had enough."

How mature is that?

Anyway, to negotiate the early stage of a new relationship, I have broken it down into some key things *not* to do:

DO NOT EMPHASIZE SEX. Certainly there is a physical attraction that brought you together in the first place. As a woman, you should stay clear of that conversation until you reach a point of total comfort and interest. If your goal is to grow the relationship into a serious one, sex should not be a priority. As great as sex and intimacy are, engaging in them too early clouds things. You want him attracted to all of you—your mind, heart, and soul in addition to your body.

It is ridiculous to set a hard and fast rule on how long you should wait before sex. As an adult, you just have to use your good judgment based on the things that are important to you.

On top of that, if you throw sex into the equation too quickly, he could very well look at you in a light you do not want. Men can be very particular, and if you are too loose, so to speak, he could determine that to mean that you are loose with most any man. And that's the death of a potential relationship. He might continue to hang around, but in his mind, the relationship maxed out around the time you slept with him a week after knowing him.

DO NOT LOOK FOR A LABEL SO QUICKLY. Ask any man and he'll tell you that he's experienced a woman saying to him after a short time of dating, "So what are we doing?" Or, "So what do I call what we're doing?"

That's really not cool. If you have open conversations, you should be able to determine his intentions—at least to some degree—without asking that question that makes most men cringe. And he cringes because he's thinking: *I'm not even sure I like you just yet and already you're asking, 'What are we doing?' Just relax.*

I can't explain why a woman just *has* to ask that question. It's really pointless because the man generally does not have an honest answer. And you know why? Because he doesn't know. He's still feeling you out. And when he gets that question, especially relatively early in the getting-to-know stage, it makes him feel like you have serious ambitions instead of letting things evolve with ease. In a lot of cases, you might get an answer you really do not want to receive. Or you will get an answer he thinks you want to hear. Either way, it is not helpful to you.

There is great value in letting things take shape—and in showing a comfort level in your new friend by not posing questions he likely cannot (or does not want to) answer.

THIS IS TONY, MY... It is perfectly all right to introduce your new man as "Tony." He doesn't have to be called, "My boyfriend, Tony." Introducing him that way to your friends could come off as insecure, as if you're intent on letting everyone know you have a man.

Because they are your friends, they should know the nature of your relationship. You don't have to hammer them over the head with it. In fact, if you start a new relationship that is going well, it would be wise to share your general happiness about it. But to constantly tell them about every nice thing he does for you or says to you could come off as bragging, which you do not want.

It's a shame you have to contain your glee about your relationship. But we know that sometimes even our closest friends have trouble digesting all your happiness—especially when they are not happy themselves.

To keep the peace and the friendship, it's probably better to share bits and pieces of your joy and not an entire serving.

MAKING A WAY. Men are more sensitive than you think. There's always talk about a man making the first phone call and also making that check-in call the day after sex. But it definitely serves a purpose for you to call him as much as he calls you.

He likely is not keeping score, but he surely is aware if the only time you communicate is when he initiates it. He could begin to think you consider him an afterthought. That's not a comfortable place for him. Just as you like to feel secure, he does, too. So, a properly timed phone call or even a text message would go a long way toward letting him know where he stands with you.

BITE YOUR TONGUE. You like him. A lot. He has taken you to a place of expectation and promise. You're attracted to him, his mind and heart. You love him.

All that is great—but when telling a man you love him, there are a few things to consider. One, it cannot come too soon. It comes too soon and he believes you're advancing the relationship too quickly to fulfill a goal. He could take your expression of love to mean you already have him fitted for a tuxedo, wedding and children. Seriously. Two, you should have an idea of how he feels about you before you drop those three words on him. You do not want to say, "I love you" and then hear crickets. That would be an awkward position for both of you.

Instead, you might be better served saying things like, "My feelings for you have grown from when we first met." Or "I like the way we are getting to know each other. It makes me feel closer to you all the time."

Comments like those open the door for him to express himself about you, which gives you an idea of where his head and heart are. There's nothing worse than saying, "I love you," to someone and that person does not feel the same way. So, early in the relationship, even if you know how you feel, hold back on sharing those intimate feelings until you know him better—or hear it first from him.

THANKS, BUT NO THANKS: It might be hard to resist, but do not get into a habit of allowing a man to buy his way into your heart. If he's constantly trying to purchase things for you, it's his way of deflecting his deficiencies. In other words, you're so caught up in the next gift you hardly notice that he isn't really your type.

And that goes for meals or cocktails, too. So many women I have met or experienced will let me pay for every single meal or drink. As a gentleman, you should take care of the initial costs of dates. It's part of the deal. But let's say you're on your eighth time out in two months. If you think it's proper not to at least offer to pay for the drinks or dinner, then you're really sadly mistaken.

I have heard of men getting into arguments with women over this issue. Some women believe the man should always pay, as if there is a fee to being with her. It is a horrible position.

A woman who says to a man, "I'd like to take you to dinner next week-end," gets brownie points for months. And it's truly not so much about the money as it is about the gesture. Dating is very expensive for the man, and it gives him a better feeling about you if you understand this by treating him on occasion.

For men, it is imperative not to get into a pattern of buying your way into her heart. You may have purchased a tasteful gift in the early stages of dating, but now that you both feel there is a future together, it's time to put away the plastic every time you see some nice jewelry.

In addition to that, you're actually wasting your money, spending it irresponsibly on her instead of saving up for something extremely significant—like your future. If you make sound decisions about what to get her at opportune times, the presents will mean more to her and will leave less of a dent in your bank account. Steer clear of showering her with presents early on so that she doesn't get used to the "princess" treatment.

KEITH'S KEY: Managing a relationship with a man is not so much about what to do as it is what *not* to do. It would be great or easier if men did not have as many hang-ups or were not equally sensitive as women. But we are. We will not admit it, but that is the case.

This chapter boils down to making sure the man respects you. That's why you do not delve into sex too quickly. He'll respect you more because you are lady enough to make sure you get sexually involved with someone only after you really know that person and have gained a comfort level.

Do not be a typical woman who wants to accelerate the relationship, who asks, "What are we doing?" a month into meeting, who does not offer to treat the man to a meal or cocktails. Those are womanly acts that will separate you from the pack.

CHAPTER TWENTY-SIX

HIS CHILDREN, YOUR ISSUES

Dating a man with children can be a lot to handle. It requires special sensibilities. You have to be especially patient, understanding and supportive. And even with that it still could be troublesome depending on the kids and the man's mentality toward your role in their lives.

I know women who said they'd rather not deal with a man with kids because of how complicated it can get. But if you meet a man and make a connection with him, it would be a shame to pass on him because he has offspring.

So, what, then, would be important in making this work? You guessed it: communication. You really have to talk this through so there is no misunderstanding about priorities, boundaries or expectations.

Understanding each other's expectations, boundaries, parental roles, and priorities can help you decide if the relationship is worth pursuing and/or strengthen it.

Single fathers, particularly those with young children, are often open to someone who can help them raise his kids. A woman who can cook, clean, fold laundry, and provide unconditional love and support makes an ideal mate. In his mind, family is first because the kids are so important. The relationship responsibilities run beyond the typical time and care of maintaining a monogamous relationship.

On the other hand, many of today's women are career-oriented and may not be so ready to jump into a ready-made family. There is so much to overcome. It's really about the woman who dates a man with children asking the tough questions about his expectations of her.

There are certain things the woman who marries her high school sweetheart never has to worry about, and dating men with children is one of them. But the longer you date, the older the pool of men. Women who continue dating into their twenties and thirties will likely be faced with the dilemma of navigating around a man's children at one point or another, and as we get older, most of us see this as less and less of a drawback. After all, being given the opportunity to witness how a man interacts with his children gives you a sneak peek into how he would interact with yours.

First and foremost, the children come first, and you should be happy if you see that in him. If he's pawning off the kids to family and friends frequently to socialize and/or spend time with you, that is not a good sign of his commitment. But if he is on it, you must come to the understanding that you will not be the No. 1 priority in this man's life—and you should not ever want to be. Just as you would want the father of your children to place priority upon them, you should admire and respect this man's ability to make his own kids the most important people in his life. Dates may be canceled and, from time to time, plans may require rearranging, but any man who would place your needs above those of his children is probably not a man you would want to wind up with in the end.

Take your time meeting the kids. Since they are such a big part of his life you may find yourself itching to ingratiate yourself to them, but go slowly. Make sure this is a man you truly see a future with before involving his children. They have likely faced plenty of heartbreak in their short lives (regardless of the reason for their father not being with their mother), and they don't need to become attached to one more person who isn't going to be around for long. Meeting the children should be placed right up there on the evolving relationship ladder with moving in together. It really is taking everything up a notch.

The children come first. Yes, this is a repeat rule, but it is one that needs to be re-learned once you are actually a part of the children's lives. It is likely that you may not instantly connect with his kids. He may have a teenage daughter who makes her distaste for you known, or a little boy who is clearly not a fan of sharing his daddy. You may find your feelings hurt, or your temper start to flare, but in the end, the kids still come first. The best thing you can do is slap a smile on your face and keep trying. Don't allow yourself to become frustrated with them, because they are just confused kids after all. Be calm, and supportive, and consistent. If you don't allow yourself to deviate from the "children come first" mentality, they will likely eventually come around. They are just testing you in the beginning, and you have to be patient in order to pass that test.

Dating a man with children can have its own hurdles, but it can also be filled with plenty of rewards. Children see the world so much differently than we do, and if you don't have kids of your own, this could become an opportunity to really test the waters and find out if motherhood is for you.

It's likely that you will eventually become more attached to those kids than you would have ever expected, and in those cases breakups can be even harder than normal. It's just one more reason to take your time when entering into this relationship, because when kids are involved, your heart will likely also become that much more involved as well. If you can make it work, though, you may find yourself happier than you could have imagined with a man who just has that much more love to share.

Being with a man with children is never an easy thing and it isn't for the faint of heart. Don't feel bad if you can't deal with the division of attention. Take some time alone to make sure this is what you want. It's not wrong to do that. It's the right thing to do. Those kids will be a part of his life always, so you cannot take any of this lightly.

BE UPFRONT. Sometimes discussing how you are feeling will not only make you feel better, but it will let him know how you are feeling. Granted, you can't whine about every little thing, but holding back serves no good purpose. And once he knows what you are feeling, he is more prone to make adjustments to make the situation more tenable. At the very least he will respect you for communicating your feelings to him.

DEAL WITH THE BABY MOMMA (IF SHE'S AROUND AND SANE). Don't become best friends (your man could feel like he is being double-teamed) but don't make enemies with the mother of his children. It would only add tension to an already delicate situation. And it's all right to ask your man about his relationship with her. Just inquire—don't accuse. Asking about their breakup could provide some insight into how to proceed with her in dealing with their children.

MEET THE KIDS AFTER A RELATIONSHIP HAS BEEN ESTABLISHED. You do not want your man to put his kids in front of you until you are sure about what you have. It could be confusing to the kids if they are young and send the wrong message if they are older. Don't forget that every relationship is different and your children may appreciate knowing the person that their parent is dating, especially in cases where the children are older.

DON'T TALK DOWN TO THE CHILDREN. They know what is going on. Being overly nice will set off warning bells. Sit down with the kids. Tell them that you are really nervous about meeting them, because you really love their father. But—most importantly—you don't ever want to give them the impression that you are there to replace their mother. Emphatically state that you know you could never take her place, but you will always be there if they need support. Tell them you don't want to change anything about the way they've been running their lives, their family traditions, or their relationship with either their father or mother. Tell them that you may need some help learning those traditions. Finish up by telling them that you're really looking forward to getting to know them better and be open to questions.

DON'T BE UPSET IF THE CHILDREN ARE NOT INITIALLY WARM TOWARD YOU. It could be for one of the reasons above, but kids sometimes are very open to anyone nice to them and sometimes they are wary of newcomers. Or they are cold and distant despite anything you do or don't do. As the adult, you have to manage the relationship gracefully and talk to the children with respect. If the mother is around, you can bet the kids' allegiance will be toward her and they will view you as an outsider who is trying to take their daddy away. That's why you have to be graceful and patient. Do not try to act like their mother or even an authority figure—at least at first. Become someone who offers help when needed and makes them smile and feel good around you.

Let them know you have a lot to offer because of your age and experience, but that you are in tune with what's going on in their world. Kids often have warped views of their parents because they are so close to them that it is difficult for them to see them as cool or funny. You can help shed light on their father while learning more about them. The more interaction you have between them, the more you learn about them.

And of course, the more you learn about them, the easier it is to deal with them because you learn what they do and don't like. That gives you a huge advantage because you can play to their weaknesses—or strengths, depending on how you look at it.

The idea initially should not be to become their stepmother, but to become someone they trust and enjoy seeing. But even with that, there is a balance because you should not want to get so close that they do not respect you as an authority figure.

If you get too close, they'll treat you as a sister or a family friend who can be dismissed at any time because respect has not been established. The way to do so is, if given the opportunity by the father, institute some house rules that are lenient but place you in a position of authority. As an example, if you are asked to watch the kid(s) one night until late, you have to establish a bedtime. And when that time comes, make sure they hit the sack at the designated time, even if they resist. They will then look at you as more than a family friend, but also as someone who is an elder and deserves respect.

The other way to gain the children's trust and respect is to really be there for their father. Kids may be kids, but they can sense when someone is disingenuous. So, how you interact with their father around them will be vital.

It's not a good thing to ever whine your way to what you want, but it is even worse when you do it in front of a man's children. They'll view you as manipulative and sneaky. The same goes for how you communicate with him. You should never be demanding and controlling, but being that way toward him in front of his children really embarrasses him and makes you look like Darth Vader. Don't do it.

Also, you should wait quite a while before you are too touchy-feely with the father in front of his children. You do not know the lingering effect of the separation from the mother; they may resent seeing someone overly affectionate toward their dad.

KEITH'S KEY: You have to look at a man's children as his everything. Put them ahead of yourself—it's the right thing to do and the smart thing, if you want to establish a relationship with them and keep one with him. Parents are protective of their children, so the fact that he has allowed you to meet and be around them means he thinks highly of you. Do not misuse that trust. Understand that your position is to offer advice when you think it is warranted, but to not force your views on how he should raise his children. Be a support system and gradually build a relationship with his kids through kindness and a genuine nature.

CHAPTER TWENTY-SEVEN

LETTING GO OF RELATIONSHIP BAGGAGE

P art of putting yourself in a position to find love is about checking the baggage from previous relationships. We all have some residuals from a breakup that linger and can infest what's next for us if we don't get it under control. And that's not necessarily easy.

But it can be done. First of all, you have to have a commitment to break free of it. Some people get off on having something to complain about, no matter how long ago any drama took place. These are the people who are generally unhappy with their lives and they are okay with being relatively miserable or out of sorts. It would be great if they were happy, but it's not so bad that they have something to complain about.

These are the people I try to avoid—and you should, too. Who wants to be around someone whose attitude focuses on the negative? If that baggage was released, I believe you would see a different person. And so, here are some ways to get beyond the hurt from a previous relationship(s):

1. ADMIT YOUR ISSUES: Everyone wants to be considered perfect but none of us are. So, it's all right to admit our shortcomings. That's the first step to exercising the negative emotions that end up turning into fear. Don't lie to yourself. Just admit how you feel. Trying to brush aside how you truly feel does nothing to help you get better.

Don't get me wrong: Admitting it is not the same as accepting it. It's just that you need to admit it in order to move on to address it. Make sense?

2. SEEK POSITIVE SUPPORT: You know if you are carrying any negative emotions from past experiences or events, so no one should have to tell you that. But if you find that you have had the same issue more than once of not being able to shake the drama from the past, solicit a friend, family member,

or even an impartial person, who can give you some perspective. Many people believe in professional therapy, but that should be taken only if you will adhere to the advice. I know a woman who went to a family psychologist to discuss her behavior on one condition: If the therapist confirmed her feelings about the man, she should end the relationship. If she indicated that the woman had deep-rooted issues that needed to be addressed, she would address them.

Well, after an hour-long session, the doctor told the woman she was "blocking her blessings" and that she identified issues with her that she believed required more sessions. Instead of holding up her end of the agreement, the woman's response was: "What about him?" The doctor said, "No, it's you who needs to come in for one-on-one discussions."

Even at that, the woman said, "Y'all making me out to be crazy."

Needless to say, with that approach that there was nothing wrong with her, their relationship eventually floundered and finally failed.

3. BE REFLECTIVE. Figure out how you got to a place of bitterness and distortion. Why? So you will know how to not revisit it, that's why. Sit down and think about your previous relationship from the perspective of an observer. What caused you the most hurt? What do you resent about the relationship? What, in general, observation did you make about relationships and the opposite sex? Why are you angry with your former partner? Are you angry with yourself?

Yes, this could be a bit painful. And embarrassing. Painful because you were hurt and/or disappointed by what took place. But you could also become embarrassed because usually there were tell-tale signs that you likely missed that are so apparent to you now. Still, being transparent and honest opens you up to healing and discovery. If the situation was dramatic enough, you will be able to remember many of the details, which would be important in you figuring out where you went wrong and how to not travel that path again.

4. UNDERSTAND WHAT YOU WANT. Sometimes, getting what we do not want helps us understand exactly what works for us. It's a shame to get there through that route, but it happens more times than any of us realize.

But once we do get there, we cannot accept anything less than what we truly want. It makes no sense to get rid of the baggage and then fall into something that does not fit what you desire. You might not even understand how big a statement that last one is. It's big because most people actually do not know what they want. And that leads to accepting anything from anyone.

I know many, many smart women who have gotten involved with men or situations that are dumb. Married men. Men in relationships. Men of no honor. And on and on. And when I hear about these situations, it blows my mind. But it all comes down to them not really knowing what they wanted in a mate and accepting anyone who came along. Not a good look.

5. BE PATIENT. You are not going to get over a relationship disappointment in a day and you will not find an ideal mate in a day. Or week. Or month. That's just how it is. There is no telling when any of that will happen, but in the meantime, you cannot force it. Letting go of relationship baggage is a marathon, not a sprint. You have to ride it out, take on the hilly terrain and make your way to the finish line in your own time.

Finding an ideal mate requires even more patience. The way the social world is, you will meet men on a daily basis, at the car wash, in the grocery store, at the mall, in church, at work, at the park, at the club, at the zoo... wherever. But you have to be discerning and patient and allow that right person for you to come along. He will help you get rid of your baggage without even trying or knowing it because he'll be right for you. But you have to let it happen—not force it.

6. GOOD-BYE MEANS GOOD-BYE. Often, that person who caused you so much drama tries to find his way back into your life. Sometimes it is subtle— a phone call "just to say hi" or a text message. But do not fall for it. Remember how you got to where you are and that he played a big role in it.

Sometimes, the guilt eats them up and they want to make amends to clear their conscience. But it is too late—you have moved on and you have committed to relinquishing yourself from all the wounds he inflicted.

And sometimes they are sincere about being sorry and wanting a chance to make it up to you. You would have to decide on that. But if you find that you have been emotionally scared by someone, allowing them back into your life—no matter how much you might still care for them or how sincere they might sound—is a risk that might not be worth taking. Not if you are trying to move on and advance yourself and how you deal with people.

7. HOLD NO GRUDGES. It has been said to forgive is not really about you; it's about the other person. You don't need to condone either your partner or your own past behavior in order to forgive. Forgive your ex for not being able to love you the way you deserve to be loved. Acknowledge the increased learning he gave you about what you do deserve.

Forgiving him for his wrongs frees up both your mind and heart from the experience. But you don't forget. I heard a sermon once where the pastor said you should actually pray for those who do wrong by you because it lifts the burden off of you and back on to them. And it makes sense—and it works.

Plus, it does you no good to walk around with animosity in your heart. I'm not saying you should be buddy-buddy with someone who has really messed over you. But I'm saying let it go so you can go on. It clutters your mind and heart when you carry grudges. It limits your progress.

8. TAKE RESPONSIBILITY. Could everything be the fault of your ex? Did you contribute to the challenges or unhappiness of the relationship? This is not about blaming yourself. It's about being honest and seeing the bigger picture, which could empower you to move forward with a clearer idea of how to function in your next relationship. If you cannot admit your role in the failure of the relationship, then perhaps you are not looking at the full scope of the relationship. Even if you were faithful and treated him right, you are responsible in some way if you accepted behavior that was unacceptable. That's called being an enabler. So, while you might have done everything right that you were supposed to do, if you did not seek to stop bad behavior, you contributed to the downfall.

But it is all right to take responsibility. That's mature and the right thing to do. It will also help you release at least some of the animosity you might be holding.

9. FOCUS ON THE POSITIVE. Place your attention on what you want in the future and not what has happened in the past. That is turning negatives into positives. That's a state of mind that has to be your focal point. Visualize yourself in a place of comfort and peace. You will not forget what happened to you in the past—I'm not saying that. But focus on those things that make you feel good, even if it has nothing to do with a man. If you like bowling, go and bowl. If you like reading, read. If you like to take walks in the park,

walk. Indulge in all of the things that make you feel good. Only positives come out of positive acts.

10. PURGE. If you were in a serious relationship, you no doubt have things around your home that remind you of him. It's a good idea to remove the photos of him on the dresser, store away mementos that used to have value. Anything that is a constant reminder of him should go.

If you lived together, maybe move the furniture around to give the place an unfamiliar feel. Leaving your living environment the same cannot be good. The idea is to make a fresh start with a fresh mind. It can only help.

Again, do not return the inevitable phone calls or pledges of love you will receive. You might not want to go so far as to change you number, but you certainly can block his number on your cell phone. His tactic will be to wear you down with incessant contact, and he surely will talk about your good times to get you to soften your stance. Don't. Get him out of your system so you will not carry toxic feelings with you.

KEITH'S KEY: Baggage is hard to get rid of because it is heavy and can be large. But we must in order to see brighter days. These steps, worked together, offer the best chance to free yourself of any lingering effect of a relationship gone bad. It's a little tricky to not blame yourself and yet accept some responsibility at the same time, but that's what has to be done. When you do what you know is right by a man, that is all you can do. When you know he's not doing right by you, you have to call him on it and demand something different. If you don't, you are essentially enabling his bad behavior. And you know as well as I do that people will only succeed in accomplishing what you allow them to do.

CHAPTER TWENTY-EIGHT
BREAK UP TO WAKE UP

know a guy who says, "The hardest thing to do is to break up with a black woman. It never ends. You're always in this back-and-forth thing." He might be right, but there are many reasons why. One is that even though a breakup occurs and there is so much anger involved, once you settle down, at least one party feels like the issue could be overcome.

There's also the idea that one, or even both, do not like the idea of being single, or starting over. So they figure let's make up since they're already familiar with each other and already have invested so much time together.

And then there are those who like to break up, just because making up can be so intense. Whatever the case, breakups come from fights or something really ugly. In making up after a fight, it is important to understand why you were in a fight in the first place. Did you fight fairly? Did you say really harmful things to get under your mate's skin? Were you on the offense or defense?

Fights are inevitable; it's a natural part of relationships. It's just a matter of how intense they are—and we're talking verbal fighting, not physical fighting—and how well you respond to them.

Usually, fighting stems from wanting to prove the other person wrong or from some disagreement about behavior, philosophy, actions or words. Making up will be about all of that. You have to be wrong to want to make up. However, you should not continue to prove your mate wrong when trying to get things back in line. Hopefully, you come to the conclusion of making up rather quickly, because the longer animosity festers, the worse it can feel.

Of course, fights can be avoided altogether if we find a way to exist without offending each other, disregarding each other, insulting each other and generally mistreating each other. But when they do happen, the goal should be to not allow them to escalate into something to the point where there is a breakup.

But it happens. And when it does, there are methods to bring it back together.

1. BE ABOUT RESOLVING THE ISSUE. The worst thing that could happen would be to spend time justifying why you were so mad. In the scheme of things, that does not matter because you want to get past it. Don't start to give reasons for why you were fighting or you will restart the fight.

2. WHO CARES WHO WAS RIGHT? Is proving you were right more important than gaining peace between you and your mate? It shouldn't be. There will come a time when you can address the issue. But when you are trying to put the fire out is not the time. Focus on the reunion.

3. APOLOGIZE. "I'm sorry." Two words with a lot of meaning and significance but are hard for people to say sometimes. It is not a way of diminishing your points in the argument. But it is a concession that says you want to make up and that you are sorry for the drama and whatever role you played in it. That's the grown up thing to do.

4. TAKE DEEP BREATHS. You can only truly attempt to make up after you have calmed down. Do something that relaxes you, whether it's listening to soothing music, watching a movie, or applying for a job. Whatever lowers your blood pressure, do it. It will give you a clear head and heart from which to have a calm conversation about reconciliation. You cannot do that when you're still boiling over.

5. SHOW YOUR AGE. In other words, act like a grown-up. If you want to make up, be the bigger person, the mature person and handle it with grace. At the same time, if your partner does not want to be mature, do not let his position influence your actions. Remain a grown-up and do not let his shenanigans push you to a place that will not help the making-up process. Over time, your mature approach will rub off on him, and he will stop and speak to you in the same manner you have spoken to him.

6. GIVE CREDIT WHERE IT IS DUE. Amid the arguing you could have heard a valid point or two from your man. Seems to me you should acknowledge that in the make-up conversation. Admitting the strengths of his position is

not the same as backing down off your positions. Don't do that. Don't even defend your position—unless he just demands it. Giving him credit might compel him to do the same with you. But do not count on it and do not do it to receive the same from him.

7. SMILE. He could be so angry that he continues to lobby verbal attacks your way, even in the supposed make-up period because he's so intent on being right. Handle it with class. Two people yelling only does one thing—makes a lot of noise.

Stay positive even as your mate fires away with verbal assaults. Instead of igniting the situation, douse it. At the very least, do not join in on the attack. Of course, sometimes not responding makes people even angrier. But it is better to be calm and hope that he adopts your disposition.

8. TAKE HEED TO HIS POINTS. He actually could have a valid point or two in his case, you know. But the only way to know is to actually listen to what he has to say. That's only fair, right? This is not compromising your principles. If the criticisms were valid, then acknowledging them will be appreciated by him, which will help you get to the desired destination.

9. EXPRESS YOUR HEARTFELT FEELINGS. Saying "I love you" is a great way to disarm someone angry at you. And since you mean it, it would not be conning him; only letting him know that you love him so much that, even in heated moments, you do not mind saying it. To make it even better, add (but only if you believe): "This relationship is important to me and I don't like to be so mad at you, or see you so mad at me."

Again, the idea is to be upfront about how you feel. If he does not react accordingly, at least you did what you felt. Sometimes, especially when we are angry, we fail to do what we know is right. Rather, we let the other emotion—anger—rule and we end up making things even worse.

10. GIVE HIM HIS SPACE. As badly as you'd like to get beyond the breakup stage, he might be the type that needs to maintain his anger or his position for a while before he relaxes and views things differently. My experience is that with people like that, it's best to let them simmer a while. They will come around when they are ready.

Also, they do not want to feel pressured to give in to your desires when they are that way. So, trying to force it only will heighten their irritation.

Usually, men like to have their space after a breakup, but I've known women to be the same way.

11. STAY THE COURSE. Once you and your partner make agreements of what changes will be made and how you will go forward with the relationship, abide by them. Many people say anything they think will work to get back together. And once they get settled into the relationship again, they forget all about what they agreed to and slide right back into their old ways. You must respect and abide by what you mutually agreed to. If you don't, I bet you'll be facing another breakup.

12. DON'T USE SEX AS A WEAPON. Though it may feel fantastic to make up with sex, it should not become a habit. If you make love to smooth things out every time after a fight and breakup, you will find yourselves no longer being able to get turned on without having a conflict first, which is hazardous for the relationship.

13. MAKE THE ROMANCE SIZZLE. Make sure your romance stays exciting and hot throughout the relationship, not just when you kiss and make up. If you continuously show your romantic interest in your partner and vice versa, the two of you will focus on the things you love about each other instead of the things you may dislike. The idea should be to remain made up. The best way to do this is to never stop communicating. If you talk about what you are feeling and ask your partner how she or he feels about certain things, then your relationship will remain open to new ways to improve it and keep it healthy.

IMPORTANT POINTS

If your relationship was on stable ground, it is likely your breakup will not last long. The tendency is to reunite, even with bad relationships. With a good one, a breakup could be considered a mere bump in the road. But if you think you have a solid relationship and the breakup lasts for an extended period, then maybe you overestimated what you had—or that there are some other issues that need to be addressed.

At the same time, if this blowup is just one in a series of blowups, then maybe you're in an unhealthy relationship and making up should not be an option. That's something for you to access with a clear mind and heart—and not through a prism of fear of loneliness.

It's possible to hit a point of "no-return," where nothing you do seems to work in making up and getting back on track. At that point, one of the partners generally starts thinking of ending or leaving the relationship.

TOO LATE???

Sometimes, when there has been a lack of communication or angry communication after a breakup, it is easy to believe your mate has decided to resist reconciling and is ready to truly move on. That does not mean it is truly over. Not really. I have had cases where I wanted to get back together with a woman, but she wasn't having it. And just when I told myself it was "a wrap," she came around.

Here's my point: If you want to save your relationship, never agree that you should break up. He might say, "This is the right thing to do," or "We shouldn't be together anymore." Fine. If you do not agree with that position, do not respond, "Okay, you're right." You have to take pride and ego out of the equation. It's not about "sweating" or pressuring someone into a relationship. You have a different perspective about what you have with this person because you are looking at it in a calm, clear way. He still could be harboring anger that prevents him from seeing beyond his anger.

He's saying one thing, but you really do not know how concrete his decision is. He's still talking to you; if he were truly done, why spend time doing that? Now, he could feel you deserve hearing it from him. Or he could be hoping to hear the right thing from you to make him reverse himself.

So, again, do not say anything you do not feel. Once you do that, you cannot retrieve the words and backpedal. Also, if you are wrong and you know it, and if you have repeatedly been doing damage to the relationship, you should understand your man's hesitancy to get back with you. You've put him in a bad position. And even if you have truly decided to change and make it right, your apologies have been heard so often, they carry little weight.

You have to prove your commitment through other means. Depending on the violation, you have to seek out professional help, counseling or even a certified relationship coach. Ask him to join you, to show how serious you are about the change you want to make to save your relationship. If your issue is, say, smoking. He just cannot take it any longer. He views it as vile and smelly and the fact that you won't even try to give it up means that his feelings matter little—on that issue and others.

What do you do, then? If he means that much to you, you give up smoking, as hard as it may be. But you do more than that. You say, "Okay, baby, I will quit. I promise. But I'm going to need your help."

Now he has a vested interest in joining your kick-the-habit campaign.

WE'RE ON THE SAME TEAM.

Part of the problem with breaking up is that one or both of you can take the position that either is the enemy. That person feels—justifiably or not—that the other does not want to see her/him blossom and pushes arguments to actually create disharmony in that person's life.

You might think that's far-fetched, but I have talked to enough people on my radio show to tell you that it is not. There is a resentment toward the person that really clashes with the love for that person. Not quite a love/hate relationship, but close.

How do you identify the resentment? If your man points out every flaw or mistake—little or big—you make, that could be a sign. If he shows little empathy when something does not go your way, that could be a sign. Not good, right?

So, how do you overcome the resentment? You say what needs to be said: "Baby, we're on the same team. In fact, I'm your biggest fan, no matter what. I have your back—about anything."

That's a show of commitment, appreciation and respect that anyone would embrace, coming from the person they are involved with. Everyone wants to feel secure in the person in their life and that their back is being watched by them.

I know an author who has written great books. But the women he was involved with for six years did not read any of them. Does that make any sense? That's like me being involved with a woman who does not listen to my music, at least occasionally. That's not about ego at all. It's about being connected and showing that you are on your man's team. Simple as that.

But back to your mistakes being pointed out. No one is perfect, right? So why would you think your man is perfect? I wrote much earlier that you have to be about solutions, not problems; focus on positives, not negatives. To harp on someone's mistake does nothing to make it better, and we have to be about making it better. Don't say, "Keith Sweat said to ignore it when I make a mistake." That's not what I'm saying. I'm saying we all make mistakes and it is all right and probably best to talk to someone about the mistake that was made.

But there is no need to relive it over and over and over. It gives the feeling that you are not on his team and almost like you are basking in his mistakes (and vice versa). Say what you need to say and then be about correcting it. Period. That's how you show you are functioning as one and how you actually *avoid* breakups.

Seeing your partner as a fallible human being and not as an enemy will increase your ability to have compassion rather than anger, and will allow love to continue to grow in your heart—even if sometimes all you get from your partner is the "angry face." Loving someone never has been easy, but it brings many rewards. Love gives meaning to our lives and fills up any emptiness we feel.

KEITH'S KEY: Breakups will happen, some longer than others, some for a day or two. It is just part of the deal. I know a guy who had a nasty breakup with his woman. He changed his relationship status on Facebook to read, "Single." She immediately sent him an e-mail. "So why you put that on your page? People do get back together."

He was stunned because she was so absolute in her wanting nothing more to do with him. But while she was spewing so much venom, she was hoping for a reconciliation—and they ended up getting back together.

The best thing to do is to work hard to avoid the drama that comes with breakups. Form a team with your mate and make it unbreakable. If you do something that makes your man say, "I'm gone," do not accept it as his final decision. Point out the good you have in you and the good in the relationship. Admit your contribution to the situation and vow to do better through professional help, if needed. Breaking up is hard to do, but it does not have to be hard to overcome.

CHAPTER TWENTY-NINE

CHEATERS NEVER WIN—SO WHY DO IT?

It seemed like all my young life I believed what I heard, which was that it was the men who were the dogs. As I got older, that idea was confirmed by the many men I encountered and knew—and my own, uh, free spirit when it came to women.

It is a real shame because that behavior damaged many ladies who did not deserve that. What I have learned in my adult years, however, is that dogs come in both genders. Women are much more discreet about their escapades, but I see more and more—in my life, my friends' and the thousands of people I talk to regularly on the radio—that the gap is closing. And fast.

Of course, there is nothing that can kill a relationship faster than an affair. It breaks down the core element of a successful relationship: trust.

But instead of it going the other way, I believe people are cheating more and more—and it's even easier to do now than ever because of technology.

I read somewhere in 2011 about Facebook being a leading cause for relationship breakups because people go to the social media site and socialize. Men and women either meet or they make new acquaintances online and it's on after that.

It's so rampant that I have heard from men who have been targeted by women on Facebook. There is something about not being face-to-face that gives people courage to say things that they might not otherwise say. And that courage to communicate turns into courage to act out on fantasies.

This is happening as much with women as it is with men, which is a sign of the times changing along with technological advances.

Think about all the men and women who have gotten busted by someone reading an e-mail or text message. I mean, there are some side relationships that function almost strictly on text message communication. Well, that is, until they actually get together.

I guess a bigger issue is why people cheat. We will explore the basic reasons and some more intricate reasons that might even surprise you.

REASON NO. 1: HE IS NOT THE SAME. Temptation is heightened when your man just does not keep himself up—he looks older than he is and, worst of all, his attitude reflects his dry demeanor. The fact that you remain lively and fun makes his downfall even greater than it really is.

That used to be the male-only reason for stepping out. No longer. Women are just as visual as men—they recognize eye candy all day long. Looking is okay, but when you're starving for affection from someone who looks edible, then you begin to think about taking a bite out of that forbidden fruit.

So, if you have a man who you think might be getting antsy about your appearance, it is time to spruce up your look. Men are visual and are turned on by their woman looking sexy—even if it is a casual night out at the local Fridays or Applebee's.

Say all you want about desiring to be loved for your mind and heart and who you are as a full person. It definitely matters. But it matters less when you start to let your appearance drop off. And you can believe it is the same with women.

Is it shallow? Maybe. Okay, yes, it is. But, as I wrote very early on in the book, end up the same way you started. If you wore heels to get him, wear heels to keep him. If your body was cute and sexy, don't you think it would behoove you to keep your body cute and sexy to keep your man from wandering?

REASON NO. 2: BORED. Everyone likes a little excitement. That's code for "appreciation." If you appreciate your mate, you will initiate doing things together to keep interest high. And vice versa.

If you are more interested watching *Desperate Housewives* and *Real Housewives of Atlanta* than you are in creating a nice evening for your man, it stands to reason he will feel less of a priority. Now, a woman comes along who *does* appreciate his sense of humor or his work ethic and lets him know it. What do you think will happen? Or could happen?

In a perfect world, nothing would happen. If you are in a committed relationship, it should not matter what outside attention you receive. But this is not a perfect world, and he could view getting with another woman as a way of feeling better about your lack of interest.

Of course, this goes both ways. Women find themselves feeling devalued or underappreciated far more than men, and today's woman just is not taking it laying down —pardon the pun—anymore. Talking to them about family things—kids, school, work, bills—is hardly stimulating.

I was told about a woman who ended up divorcing her husband over that very issue. He just did not want to do anything that she wanted to do—no effort to add spice to the relationship. She liked to go to a bookstore for coffee and to browse reading materials on Monday nights. That was a night she just enjoyed getting out.

Well, he would not budge on it. That forced her to look at their relationship in its entirety, and what she discovered was that he was a boring person. He did not have the energy she had to experience life. So, she left. But before she did that, she had a drawn-out affair.

When a man shuts down in that way—basically limiting his interactions— today's woman is subject to take on outside interests far more than before. She will not only pay attention to men who show her interest, but she will enjoy it. And if the timing is right and the person says the right things, she will take that unfaithful step.

REASON NO. 3: THE N WORD. Unless you are a masochist, you want peace. You want calm. You want pleasure. There is a spoken word artist/poet in Atlanta named Hank Stewart. He explores human dynamics in his work, and his piece, "The Garage Door," speaks to this point. In a nutshell, Hank speaks about a man being at home, peaceful, relaxed—until he hears the garage door come up, indicating his woman is home. He knows her arrival indicates that his state of tranquility is about to end. "Damn," Hank says in the poem.

He wrote about how badly a nagging woman can mess up a mood. But there are more nags out there than you might guess. Your girlfriend in your book club, who always seems in control and together, could be a nag at home. Women are great at keeping their alter egos under wraps.

A nag is like a gnat—they annoy you repeatedly and incessantly until you leave. Not good, right? So, instead of being intimate with her, you're looking to get away from her—and to a place where you are appreciated and where there is peace.

REASON NO. 4: GOING IN OPPOSITE DIRECTIONS. There was a time when he would never go to the movies without you. Playing golf on Saturdays was just a twice-a-month thing, not every Saturday—and some Sundays. And he only hung out with the boys once every two months or so, just to be sociable. Now it is a regular deal.

Meanwhile, you go out for drinks more and more after work with coworkers. You used to have dinner ready for your man when he came home after Saturday golf. Now, he gets there to a note from you saying you went to visit your mother's house—and there is no food.

Getting the picture? You start to do things apart instead of together. No couple should be together all the time. But when you struggle to find time together, you open up the opportunity to meet someone new. And because you have this separation and time to be on your own, the temptation to explore the possibilities is acted on.

But here's the bigger point: If you were really into your man and he into you, moving in different circles would not be an issue.

REASON NO. 5: NO GOOD REASON...DUH. That's the sound of those who were waiting for this reason. Some people, especially men, just do not have an explanation for their cheating.

You can ask him twenty different ways and it comes back to the same thing: He has no idea.

Or, if he does, he's not saying. The thinking among men is that it is just in our DNA, a primal instinct to seek and conquer. You would think some married men—like Kobe Bryant and Tiger Woods, for example—would never think of risking their marriages and public perception by having flings with random women.

They have no rhyme or reason to it; it is just something to do. To a woman, that's just plain stupid.

You can probably detect this in your man based on a few things. How does he act at a party with you when there are several attractive women around? Do his eyes roam? Do you notice him noticing other women in more than a casual way? Is he extra-friendly around women? Those are clues that he might be a woman lover supreme and not need a reason to step out.

With those kinds of men, you have to keep him guessing about you. Sexually stimulate him in a different way. In other words, give him different experiences that will focus his attention on what's coming next from you and not another woman.

If that doesn't keep him home, you cannot blame yourself. That's truly on him.

REASON NO. 6: FLAT PEPSI. Ever pour some soda that has gone flat into a glass? What happens? Not much, right? Well, that's how it is with a relationship that has gone flat, too. You pour everything into it, but nothing happens. There's no fizz.

This malaise happens all the time. It's no one's fault, really. It just occurs over time. You could seem happy in the relationship, even. You almost don't even notice that things have deflated.

But you might be going through the everyday motions and feeling secure, but it hits you one day that you want more, that you need some excitement. You look at the person next to you in bed and he's snoring and you think: "He's not the one."

Once the romance fades, you feel like he is not the man you fell in love with. Now, the little things that bothered you some anger you a lot. You look in the mirror and decide you deserve more, even though you are not going anywhere. So you decide the parent at your son's baseball game, the dad who always goes out of his way to speak to you, is kind of cute.

And before you know it, you are excited about flirting with him, starting an affair that reenergizes your being.

REASON NO. 7: EGO, ANYONE? I wrote this earlier: Men are insecure. For all the arrogance and confidence we strut, our ego needs constant nourishment. So, even with a wonderful, loving woman, men can still seek other action to feed the ego.

Not only that, the ego has to be further fed by men sharing stories of their escapades with their closest friends. It makes them feel bigger because their friends are impressed by their exploits. This would have nothing to do with you; it would be all about him.

Meanwhile, a woman's ego needs nurturing, too. And she will get it—

from an old boyfriend, a newcomer that intrigues her—but she won't tell a soul about it. She might share with her super-duper closest friend, but that's it. Her ego is such that she does not want her friends to look at her in a negative way.

REASON 8: MEANINGLESS. You've heard it before: "It meant nothing to me," he said. She will offer, "I don't love him." That's how they explain that it's just sex, so you should not be mad at them.

Men say all the time: "I love my wife. What I do with her is totally different. It's just sex. It means nothing."

That mentality allows them to sleep with women with no conscience. In their minds, they have separated sex and making love. And as long as they aren't making love to other women, it is not bad.

There are women who adopt that same principle, and jump from man-to-man without flinching—or guilt. They are not the norm—usually, a woman could start out that way. But as she enjoys the sex, the attention and the person, she soon falls for him, creating even more drama.

In any case, those who say, "It's just sex," do not take the time to consider what it would mean to their significant other if they found out. They are selfish and go just for their own physical desires.

REASON NO. 9: PAYBACK IS A MOTHER. I know of many cases where the woman stayed with the man, but she knew in her heart she was going to cheat on him, as a way of payback.

She needed to do to him what he did to her to not feel like she was played. He might not ever find out about it. But she will have the satisfaction of knowing that he did not get over on her without her doing anything about it.

And because he cheated first, she believes she has the right to do the same. Yes, it is tit-for-tat, but she does not care. She just wants to get on a level playing field.

For the man who catches his woman cheating, well, it can be a different story. It's like men expect it from men. But when it's his woman, he cannot take knowing someone else has been there. That's the territorial nature of men—and the double-standard nature in us.

If he stays—and that's a big "if"—it would take a lot for him to look at her in the same way. Years. Decades. It would always be in his mind, lurking, eating away at him. That's just how men are. That does not make it right, especially when he wants her to forgive his infidelity in an instant and go on like nothing happened.

OVERCOMING CHEATING

So, those circumstances above—whether you agree with them or not, like them or not—are some of the reasons people cheat. How do you get beyond it?

You love the man. You see the good in him. You believe he is sorry and you want to trust that it will not happen again. Above all, you do not want to lose the relationship, despite the pain and humiliation that came with him cheating.

What do you do?

Since you feel about him as you do, you have conquered the first steps. You can't possibly get beyond the betrayal if you were iffy about your feelings.

In order to overcome the odds, you have to be patient and not rush into reconciliation because of those factors. You need really clear and open conversations about how you got to this place. You have to be honest with yourself and address the emotional pain his actions caused and express to him exactly what you felt/are feeling.

Study his responses. If you detect that he is not genuinely apologetic or sincere about his promises—or is doing so because he feels it is the thing to do—then you should really give forgiving him real consideration. The last thing you want is a man hanging around because he feels he owes it to you. You are not a charity case. He has to be into making it work as much as you.

If you sense that he is on board for trying to make it work, then you have a real opportunity to make that indiscretion something that turns your relationship into something special. There will be some turbulent times along the way. You're not going to get over his cheating quickly. Some days you will feel great about the course you are on. Occasionally, you will be hurt all over again. And angry. That's just how it is. But if things are growing as you like, then he is slowly rebuilding in you the critical element he lost—trust.

You look up "trust" in the dictionary and it will read: "A firm belief or confidence in the honesty, integrity and reliability of another person."

To regain that in you, your man will have to endure a lot, especially your mood swings about what happened. It could be six months later and he'd think things are going great. And then, suddenly, you bring up that situation again. It's going to happen.

But if he withstands that—handles the random inquiries and the attitude changes—it says a lot about his commitment to making it up to you and being the man you want him to be.

I must be honest. My experience is that most men do not stand up to that kind of pressure. At some point, they go, "I can't take this," and bounce. But that's all right. Do not let him turn the situation around, as if he's the victim. You have to stand your ground to get to a mental place of comfort.

KEITH'S KEY: Cheating happens. That doesn't make it right or acceptable. You can control what you do by either linking up with a mate that works for you, REALLY works for you, or by just doing what is right as long as you are in a committed relationship.

On the other side, take the points above about why people cheat and use them to make sure you do not fall short in your relationship. Be open and honest, attentive and adventurous, interested and exciting. If you do what you're supposed to do in a relationship, well, that's all you can ask of yourself. If he cheats anyway, you know that it is on him, not you.

We all are familiar with the warmth and *safety* trust can provide; however, we also know the intense emotional pain and agony of having experienced trust broken.

Since trust is a basic necessity in a healthy relationship, I find it rather curious that the word "us" sits comfortably in the midst of the word *trust*.

The truth is that there can be no *us* if there is no *trust*, because *trust* is one of the critical bonds that connect and endear two people to one another.

So with this as our foundation today, I'd like you to think about two questions today regarding trust:

Who do you trust the most? And are YOU trustworthy? I trust you will find these two questions a bit challenging, *insightful* and enlightening.

CHAPTER THIRTY

MEETING YOUR MATCH ONLINE

There was a story in *The Atlanta Journal-Constitution* in the late 1990s about a beautiful, single black woman who met a man on an online dating site. They courted each other for a lengthy time—I cannot remember how long—and ended up getting married in New York.

But here's the thing: She did not meet her new husband—never even saw him in person—until she walked down the aisle at their wedding. That's right. They met online, communicated for many, many months strictly online, graduated to phone conversations, but never had a real date, never hugged, never looked into each other's eyes—until *after* they were married.

The bride wrote the article, detailing her romance that started on an Internet website. In the article, she wrote that her brother and father had traveled to New York to meet her husband-to-be, and they had given him the thumbs-up, which was enough for her.

From what I understand, they remain happily married more than fifteen years later.

That's some love story, huh?

While it might be the extreme, people finding mates online has mushroomed into a huge industry. There are millions of people who not only try it, but they believe in it. You think people are obsessed with Facebook. Some of these dating sites are just as addictive.

There are dozens and dozens of various dating websites designed to put people together. Some, like eHarmony, insist they match people according to a formula rating compatibility. Whatever. Bottom line, people are finding the rat race of meeting someone "nice" difficult and use online dating/meeting as a last resort.

Obviously, like the story above and hundreds of others, there is viable reason for these websites. But here's another story:

A woman met a man on a dating site. They e-mailed each other for about three weeks and finally escalated to phone calls. Eventually, she accepted an offer to meet the man in his hometown of Atlanta. She flew in from Chicago on an early flight. Their initial meeting was cool, but she was tired from having to get up around 4:30 a.m.

So they decided to go back to his place where she would take a nap and they would then get on with the day. They arrived at his house and she said she wanted to sleep on the couch for a few hours. He set it up for her and she eventually dozed off as he handled household responsibilities.

A few hours later, she awoke, feeling refreshed and prepared to really get to know her online friend. She looked around the downstairs part of the house but did not see him. She went upstairs and called out his name, but got no response. She wandered into the master bedroom and there he was—on the floor, unconscious.

Panicked, she called 9-1-1. She tried to revive him until they arrived. They hurried him on a gurney and she gathered her purse, cell phone and his cell phone and jumped in the back of the ambulance with him and the paramedics.

A half-hour after waiting in the hospital, the doctor came out to tell her he had died. Heart attack. She was shocked and did not know what to do. Several minutes after the news, his cell phone rang. The caller was identified as "Wife."

She was taken aback because they had discussed their marital status. She answered. And, sure enough, it was his wife.

"Who is this?" the wife wanted to know.

"Well, I, uh, I'm a friend and I am at the hospital with your husband," she said to the woman. "I'm so sorry. The doctors just told me he died of a heart attack."

Not a pretty picture.

The point of that story is that you really, *really* have to be careful of who you meet on the Internet. None of what happened in this woman's case was her fault. But she was duped into believing her new friend was single when he was not.

Nevertheless, online dating services provide options for the lonely hearts or those fed up with conventional social meetings. There is no reason to believe you cannot meet a good person for you on a website. I would say the odds are close to the same as meeting someone out at a club, or church, or an event. You just don't know who you're dealing with until you deal with them.

What online dating has done is allow you to stay at home with rollers in your hair and beer stains on your shirt and meet people. If you have a smartphone, you can even make contact with potential new friends while you move about.

It would be wise to proceed with caution if you decide on this method of socializing. There is a serious element of the unknown. Those who do it contend there are serious benefits to it and even believe it will get more popular in time. I like the idea of seeing someone and making that connection in person. But that's me.

SO, ANYWAY, HERE ARE SOME BENEFITS TO ONLINE DATING:

♥ In one night, scrolling through a website, you can encounter dozens of prospects, something you cannot do in a night out with the girls. Because you both are on a dating site, there are no real awkward moments or hesitancy about approaching someone. That's why they are there.

So, you don't have to develop a pick-up line or have awkward moments that could take place when initially meeting someone.

You get to talk to the person first online and, if you find out that you are compatible, you can then find out if the chemistry sticks, even if you haven't met the person yet, by continuing your relationship online.

You can meet all different sorts of people, with different backgrounds and interests, even those located in places far away from you if a long distance relationship works for you.

♥ It is cost-effective. Men complain about the dating process and how much money they have to spend just getting to know one person. If he takes a woman out five times—three dinners, one lunch and one occasion for cocktails—he's already spent more than five hundred dollars. And that relationship might not go anywhere, even as your money evaporates.

Online, you can have twenty times the conversation you would have on five dates. You could do that in one night and it would not cost you any more than the membership of the service. And you can do that to more than one person—feel out who you really are connected to and then make a decision. You do not have to spend money on new outfits or gas. You only need a computer or mobile phone. No need to dress (or even undress) to impress, or spend hundreds of dollars for a date that will go nowhere.

❤ Some websites give you quality results. They match a detailed profile based on personality tests and even psychological quizzes. They call it scientific, but it is not an exact science. Still, if you believe in the power of having common interests, then those services might be a better fit.

Other services allow a more organic (as organic as you can be on a computer) experience, where you pay a fee to roam the site and make your introductions based on photographs or what you see from various profiles.

❤ You can set your expectations already within the website you are signing up to, or the chat room that you'll be entering, or state what you are looking for in a relationship right off the bat! Serious relationships only, on the rebound, looking for Mr. Right or Mr. Right Now, or "just playing around." There is no urgency or need to enter in a relationship where you'd have to find out that you've been fooled by a player, or you've hurt someone who was serious from the very beginning. And no need to explain yourself!

Importantly, you do not feel the sting of rejection online as you do in person. Rejection online isn't as embarrassing. Rejection through chat or e-mail, or even by simply ignoring the person who isn't very interesting, or being ignored by someone you expressed interest in, makes it cut and dry.

❤ Once you have connected with someone, you can revert to traditional methods of dating. Only you have gotten a lot of the preliminary stuff out of the way. Those who have been successful in dating online would not trade it for anything. They were careful and methodical in who they met and how they advanced the connection. And they said they are better for the experience.

THE DISADVANTAGES OF ONLINE DATING

❤ Addiction is never good, and by all accounts, surfing online dating sites can become compulsive. You can even get caught up with Internet flirting, meeting people, viewing photos and profiles. It's addictive and it's easy, a short-term remedy for loneliness or boredom. But you can find yourself on your computer for hours at a time, ignoring other responsibilities that require your attention.

❤ It is basically shooting in the dark. We judge a person's character based on what we learn, see and intuitively feel. Facial expressions, body language, even someone's smile can give us a feel for the kind of person he/she is.

With an online service, people can shape the images they want to convey, which might not be an accurate depiction. You lose all those instinctive elements we use in assessing someone. You could very well finally meet that person and he may not look or act anything like you were led to believe. Unless you get beyond the e-mail stage, the Internet is a waste of time. Lastly, dating online eliminates those who are not online seeking companionship, meaning you are limiting yourself.

KEITH'S KEY: First of all, do not go into an online service website thinking it will be the cure to all your relationship troubles. Go in with an open mind, much like you do a traditional dating situation.

Do your research on the site you choose to explore, understanding that all sites are not the same and many offer vastly different rates and options. For sure, be very wary of even the people who appear to be totally stand-up and legitimate. And when you do decide to finally meet someone in person, do so in a totally public and crowded place. Tell someone you know where you are going and let them know when you get back safely home. Again, you can never be too careful.

D o you like you? Do you like what you see? Do you like the words that come out of your mouth? Do you like the things you think? Do you like how you go about business? Do you like life?

To some people, those may seem like silly questions. But to a great many, they are legit inquiries that they struggle to answer. And those are the very people seeking love in all the inappropriate places—or they put up with nonsense in relationships that are going nowhere.

It's like this, and you've heard it before: You must love yourself before you can truly love someone else.

It makes sense, right? If you do not feel good about whom you are, you almost always will embrace anyone who shows you interest—even if that person is nowhere near what is good for us. He might have some virtues that you admire or respect. Or he may be that physical type that you desire. But really it's about being with someone, almost anyone, to feel good about yourself, to fill some hole inside you or to change what other people think of you. These relationships are doomed to failure from the start, because you aren't really into it and would have to stretch yourself just to act like it matters.

When you ask someone you're getting to know, "What kind of music do you like?" it's not just idle chatter. You ask for a reason. You are looking for compatible traits, common interests.

The right person for you has similar interests in the things that matter: politics, religion, music. Your philosophy on life, work, children, etc., will be a dead-on match or very similar. I addressed the "opposites attract" idea earlier in this book. It does not hold up when you're dealing with two people with low self-esteem issues. When there is one party that does not really believe in himself/herself, then linking with someone that is not a match…well, it's not a good look.

If you like yourself, you will like the people you naturally meet, and they will like you. If you don't like yourself, you will waste energy trying to get with people who aren't like you, or you will settle for being with someone you don't like.

SOLUTIONS

There are only two ways to go with this:

Learn to like yourself.

Evolve into the person you want to be.

This is really psychological. If you want to like yourself, one way to do it is to realize that you are the most perfect you that anyone could be. No one else can do the things you do quite like you. No one sees the world quite the same way. No one else has precisely your talents, or ambitions. No one messes things up the same way. Real talk: It's okay to be the way you are.

Once you get on board with this idea, you will start seeing others the same way. And you will put yourself in relationships with people who appreciate your quirks, strengths, weaknesses, etc.

As for transforming yourself, it is much easier to do when you accept yourself for who you are. Once you like yourself, you will see without impairment who you'd like to grow to become.

And I would be willing to bet that that person is someone who is more like you than not. I heard it explained this way before: A computer nerd falls for the cute cheerleader. But the cheerleader likes the football player. Why? It's not just because the nerd has on an ink-stained shirt. But she performs physical feats as a cheerleader and so appreciates and is drawn to the athlete who also is physical, comfortable socially and shows confidence. They have a common interest. She wouldn't want to be with a guy who locks himself in his bedroom, is anti-social, and can't look her in the eye when he speaks.

Unless the nerd is going to turn into a football player, he has no shot at the cheerleader. In truth, he wants the bookish girl who is already on his wavelength. Either way, the solution is rooted in self-acceptance.

Once you recognize who you are, you will better understand your true motives for wanting someone you can't have or shouldn't want. If you want to be with them to compensate for your own shortcomings, you will no longer want them. If you want them because you want to be like their ideal partner, then you have the confidence to embody that person. So there is never a need to change who you are for someone else.

Accept yourself, like yourself, love yourself...and you will like the potential mates that come your way. Improve yourself, and you will attract the partner you want, the partner that fits with you.

ABOUT THE AUTHOR

Keith Sweat (born in Harlem, New York) is an R&B and soul singer, songwriter and radio personality. He is the host of "The Sweat Hotel," the #1 urban nighttime radio program in the nation, which is aired in 49 markets. Sweat once worked an ordinary 9-to-5 job for the commodities market in the New York Stock Exchange. He sang at nightclubs until he was discovered in 1987. On November 25, 1987, Sweat released his debut album, *Make It Last Forever*, which sold four million copies. The biggest hit was "I Want Her" (#1 R&B), and the title track was #2 on the R&B charts. He was considered one of the early stars of the genre New Jack Swing. In 1992, Sweat discovered the group Silk, and helped craft their debut album, *Lose Control*. Its single "Freak Me" hit #1 on the Billboard Hot 100. In 1995, Sweat discovered the Atlanta-based female R&B group Kut Klose. Sweat also formed the R&B super group LSG with Gerald Levert and Johnny Gill, and released their self-titled debut album, *Levert.Sweat.Gill*, in 1997. Visit www.thesweathotel.com and www.keithsweat.com

READER DISCUSSION GUIDE

1. What does invading your mate's privacy (reading e-mails, checking cell phone) say about the strength of your relationship?

2. How important is it to not ignore warning signs when selecting a mate?

3. What is romance and why is it important in a successful, loving relationship?

4. How do you add spice in a relationship that has turned dull?

5. How do you build trust in a relationship?

6. Should you share your personal business about your mate with your girlfriend, seeking advice? Why? Why not?

7. Is communication overrated in building or maintaining a relationship?

8. In troubling times, how important is it to remain faithful and not turn to someone else?

9. How can you make dealing with the mother of your man's children something positive for all parties?

10. What's the best way to prevent your relationship from becoming boring?

11. Can you stand prosperity? Or are you always looking for the other shoe to drop?

12. Do you respect yourself enough to demand respect from your mate—and give him his proper respect?

13. How do you deal with in-law interference, relationships?

14. Do you get married because your friends are married or you're getting older, or because the man in your life moves you?

15. How do you handle financial issues that arise in relationships?

Printed in the United States
By Bookmasters